Wicked
Ulster County

Wicked ULSTER COUNTY

TALES OF DESPERADOES, GANGS & MORE

A.J. SCHENKMAN

Charleston · London

THE
History
PRESS

Published by The History Press
Charleston, SC 29403
www.historypress.net

Copyright © 2012 by A.J. Schenkman

All rights reserved

First published 2012

Manufactured in the United States

ISBN 978.1.60949.716.3

Library of Congress CIP data applied for.

Contents

In Memory of our Moms, Lorraine and Joyce.
Dedicated to my Dads.

Preface

All Things that are Wicked

I was not born in Ulster County, New York. In fact, I was not even born in the Hudson Valley but in another valley one hundred miles away called Queens, New York, named for the Queen consort Catherine of Braganza, who married King Charles II of England. It, too, had a rich history, especially Flushing. Never had I heard of places with unique names like Kerhonkson, Shawangunk, New Paltz or Napanoch, to name a few. I knew of Ellenville because of the Schrade Knife Outlet, formerly across the street from Dunkin' Donuts. It never occurred to me that I might one day be calling a small hamlet in Southwestern Ulster County my home.

Ulster County, New York, is a wonderful place to live and raise a family. Today, it is far from a wicked or violent place. It has its problems, like everywhere else in the world, but it is a good place, generally speaking. The stories in this book are, for the most part, isolated incidents that occurred over a long period of time in the county's lengthy history. These anecdotes surfaced from my research on other subjects—my attention kept getting diverted by captivating events. I took note of these stories in order to revisit them later. Before I knew it, so many interesting events had accumulated that I had the makings of an entire book. One of my favorite newspapers used for this book, and my research in general, is the *Kingston Daily Freeman* because of its extensive coverage of happenings in this area; there are other local papers that I readily consult as well.

I guess you could say that this book has been in the making for some twenty years. It started when I created my first column in the *Times Herald*

Record called "Stories on the Wind." After a hiatus from newspaper writing, the column was resurrected a few years later in the *Shawangunk Journal* as "More Stories on the Wind." These columns, and this book, were born out of my love for good stories about ordinary people becoming involved in extraordinary situations. They also permit my fascination with reading old newspapers, which has been made easier with large digital archives.

The book before you is the culmination of years of poring over old newspaper articles. Many of them are of stories or scandalous headlines that piqued my interest and propelled me to investigate some of the villains of Ulster County. I must put forth the problems that I have encountered when working from these newspapers, such as inconsistencies in stories, dates and, in some cases, actual events. In many instances, other sources were used to confirm facts as much as possible. However, many of the stories in those old newspapers were subject to interpretation not only by those writing them but also those who were interviewed. These stories should be regarded less for their historical value, though they certainly have a historic significance, than for their entertainment value. In short, one must remember that these are just stories that were found circulating in newspapers and in many cases have long since been forgotten. The only exception is the story about the burning of Kingston, which is largely based on established facts.

In a larger sense, these stories reflect a time gone by when citizens congregated at the local luncheonette, tavern or firehouse to discuss scandalous individuals or wicked stories of the day and where old men sat for hours sipping a cup of coffee and talking about the latest news or what was happening in their lives. This book is a slice of old Ulster County and a simpler time forgotten.

Acknowledgements

Special thanks to Whitney Tarella; Darcy Mahan; Jeff Saraceno; Ellenville Public Library and Museum; William Dourdis; JoAnn Dourdis; Ken Gray; *Shawangunk Journal*; John Warren Jr.; Marybeth Majestic; Jane Kellar; Lisa Spada-Bruck; Geoff Hazzard and Heather Hazzard; Marc Phelan; Carol Johnson; Tony Adamis; Carlton Mabee; Sharon Richman, who gave me her blessings for this book; Elizabeth Werlau; Eric Roth; Laura Smith; Ulster Savings Bank; Diane Hassan; Sylvia Rozzelle; Wayne Lempka; Gerry, Charlie and Kevin, for their sense of history; Cory Mitchell and Michelle Greco, who listen patiently to my writings; Heather Friedle and Andrea Durbin; Dad, Peter and to the many other individuals whom I pester, annoy, provoke and agitate to read my writings, too numerous to remember. If I have forgotten anybody, please accept my most humble apology.

CHAPTER I

Alligators in Ellenville

When driving around Western Ulster County through High Falls, or even into Sullivan County along the Old Mine Road on what is today known as US Route 209, one can still see the remnants of the once great canal system known as the D&H Canal. The ruins are just about everywhere you look. In fact, many of the names of different towns, and in some cases the towns themselves, were born out of the D&H, such as Rosendale or Wurtsburo, named for William Wurts. Even many of the local roads still bear the names of their functions when the canal was in operation: Tow Path Road, Berme Road and Creeklocks Road, to name only a few.

The initials D&H stand for the Delaware and Hudson Rivers. The canal linked the coal fields of Pennsylvania with the Hudson River, where coal was shipped to New York City. The canal was in operation from the 1820s to 1899 and ran over one hundred miles, boasting over one hundred locks stretching from Honesdale, Pennsylvania, to Kingston, New York, where the canal fed into the Hudson River. Since it ran for such a long time, there are more than a few interesting stories associated with the canal. One of the most interesting was reported by the *New York Times* in 1885.

When I was growing up in New York City, I can't remember how many times I heard stories of huge alligators roaming the sewers, subsisting on rats. Every time I walked by a storm drain with a friend, inevitably one of them would exclaim that there were alligators the size of buses wandering the sewer systems of New York City. Many scientists hold fast that alligators were never pulled alive from subterranean New York City,

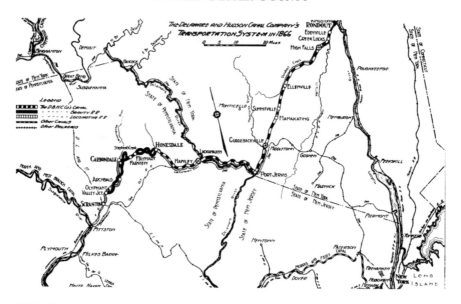

D&H Canal map. A map of the length of the D&H Canal with the towns it ran through. *Courtesy of Library of Congress.*

though sixteen-year-old Salvatore Condulucci, of 419 East 123rd Street, begged to differ in an account published in the *New York Times* on February 10, 1935. He claimed to have, with other youths, pulled an alligator from a manhole. I am a skeptic by nature, so I never really paid much mind to this urban legend, let alone to another about an alligator being pulled from the waters near Ellenville, New York, by an individual named Kelly Cook in late November 1885.

During my time as a volunteer firefighter, I have spent many nights on what is called "standby." Standby usually occurs when a neighboring fire department requests other neighboring fire departments to staff its firehouses. They do this in order to have potential firefighters available to respond to a call quicker than if the volunteers had to wait to respond to an alarm. During standby, some of the firefighters inevitably reminisce about the long-gone days. As the sun went down on one summer evening in Kerhonkson and we pulled up chairs in the doorways of our first engine bay, a senior firefighter recalled a discussion we had earlier about Lock 25 and the Little Stony Aqueduct that held my attention for over an hour.

This discussion, in turn, gave way to a discussion about the D&H Canal, which, at one time, ran down Main Street in Kerhonkson. In fact, Kerhonkson was birthed by the emergence of the canal and originally was not called Kerhonkson at all but Middleport. I sat listening with a historian's

Canal at Ellenville. The alligator was sighted not too far from here. *Author's collection.*

Kerhonkson. Canal Street, or today Old Main Street, was once, and hopefully will become again, the center of town. *Author's collection.*

ear and took mental notes, as I knew that many of these stories were not in textbooks. I went home late that night, and the next morning ensconced myself in the history of the D&H Canal. I sat in my study with a pile of books and a laptop with a determination to write a piece about the Little

Stony Aqueduct. However, I kept thinking about Cook and the alligator found in the canal system.

One of many stops on the canal was Ellenville, New York; indirectly, this place is the subject of this story, which appeared in newspapers and was also mentioned in the book *The D&H Canal: Carrying Coal to the Rondout*. According to sources, in late 1885, Cook lived in Ellenville, where he ran a boat on the D&H Canal during what was referred to as the "boating season." One particular day in November of the same year, Cook's boat was "passing over the twelve-mile level," which, according to Matthew Osterberg's book *The Delaware and Hudson Canal and the Gravity Railroad*, "started at Lock 57."

Osterberg recalls in his book that the pass was "very isolated." It was on this lonely stretch of the D&H Canal that Cook looked at something he thought was moving just under the water. He ignored it at first, though once again, he saw a large object that appeared to be swimming just under the surface. He became concerned when the object was "50 yards" from his boat. Cook called out, not being able to make out the object now swimming towards him quite quickly. In yelling out, he hoped that the "steersman" would help him ascertain this large object swimming around in the water of the canal. The job of the steersman on the canal was to keep the boat in the middle of the canal. Once he managed to grab the attention of the steersman, both men used the tow line to form a noose, eventually capturing the swimming "curiosity." It is safe to say that neither of the men expected what came next.

Once they hoisted it aboard their vessel, imagine their surprise when they discovered that they had, in fact, pulled an alligator out of the water. The reptile was roughly "3 foot" in length. When word circulated that an alligator had been sighted and caught in the D&H Canal, another story surfaced about another alligator in the canal.

Captain Thomas Gurry, of Rondout, came forth claiming to have seen an alligator "three days before," in the same spot where Cook and the steersman caught it. He tried himself to seize it. However, it eluded his attempts at capturing it by diving under water. He never saw the creature again or heard about it until Cook and the steersman caught it.

People were at a loss to explain how an alligator could end up making its home in that section of the canal or even how it survived there in the first place. Aside from the articles mentioned in the next paragraph, the story itself disappeared from the newspapers after it was reported; it seemed to be an isolated incident. By all indications in its long history, this was the only alligator caught in the canal.

Alligators. *Courtesy of Library of Congress.*

What exactly became of this curiosity is not mentioned either. The commotion that the alligator caused persisted from the last two weeks of November into December, when the story was picked up by the *New York Times.* Although finding an alligator in the canal was uncommon, owning a pet alligator was not unheard of during that time. When looking through old papers of the era, it became apparent that when vacationers traveled to Florida, they sometimes brought back alligators as pets. Sometimes these same persons brought alligators back to be given as presents.

In 1872, the *Kingston Daily Freeman* reported that an individual had placed alligator eggs under his mattress in order to hatch them. He had returned from Florida with them and at last report, they had hatched. Three years later, in 1875, the same paper reported the following: "A.H. Bruyn has been blessed by the presentation of two pet alligators. They are all mouth, with exception of a small space for the tail to be fastened on, and are the dearest little pets imaginable."

The voracious appetites of these pet alligators demanded a constant source of meat. The article went on to report that local cats and dogs that

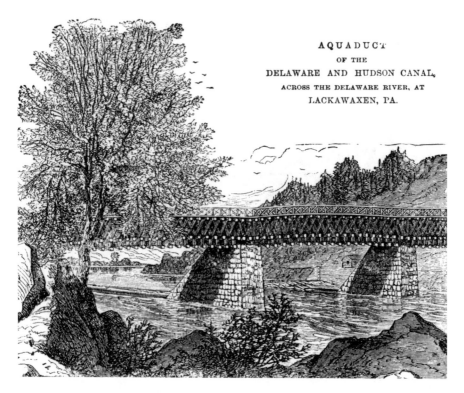

D&H Canal. *Courtesy of Library of Congress.*

no one wanted were quite a prize for these animals (which were kept behind a fence). The article reached out to the community and asked people to contact Mr. Bruyn if they had an animal they no longer wanted or strays that could be lowered over the alligators' fence. He assured people that the animals would suffer little, but they would have to be carefully lowered behind the fence by way of a rope around their tails.

So it is possible that once no longer wanted, these alligators might have found their way into local waterways as they grew too large and aggressive for their handlers. It also most likely was expensive to feed these animals enough food to sustain them. Either way, there was only one recorded instance of an alligator actually calling the D&H Canal its home, let alone surviving the cold weather of Ulster County, where the canal ran.

Rip Van Markle

Living in New York State's Hudson Valley, it is hard to escape the stories of Washington Irving. Many students first learn of this author through his short story "The Legend of Sleepy Hollow." A close second in popularity is "Rip Van Winkle," the short story of a man who falls asleep for twenty years in the Catskill Mountains. Early in 1897, the *New York Times* published a story about a "modern day" Rip Van Winkle living in the town of Rochester near Kerhonkson. Why it decided to call him Rip Van Winkle is not clear because the two did not bear much resemblance to each other, other than possibly in appearance. Even if he was not a modern-day Rip, his story is surely interesting to say the least.

George Silas Terwilliger was a cooper by trade. A cooper was an individual who made barrels. These barrels were made out of wood and required a certain amount of skill to produce. The staves had to be created by the cooper, and he might use a metal band to hold them in place. The way the barrels were constructed depended on what was to be carried within them. It was not a path to wealth, but it did allow for a steady income.

Terwilliger lived on Wilbur Street in Kingston, New York, with his wife, Elizabeth. By all indications, they were a somewhat happy couple, having been married for a long time by the 1890s. He knew that Elizabeth had been married previously to a Civil War veteran named Peter B. Markle in 1869. She, in fact, had lived with him for a time with his family in Samsonville, near Kerhonkson in the Catskill Mountains. They shared a remote home that was nothing like the one in Kingston, which was a decent-sized town. When her husband, George, became curious about her former husband, Elizabeth

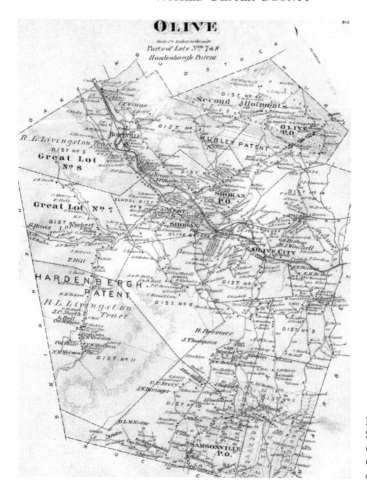

Map of
Samsonville.
*Courtesy of Ulster
County clerk's
archives.*

halted his inquisitiveness by telling him that he was dead, indicating that this was the reason that they were no longer together. This seemed to be sufficient information for Terwilliger.

Life has a way of sometimes throwing us curves, as it did in the case of George and Elizabeth Terwilliger. Sometime in the late 1890s, Terwilliger became tired of his life with Elizabeth and, according to accounts from the time period, left their home on Wilbur Street in Kingston. He had met a young woman who lived in New Paltz at the base of the Shawangunk Mountains. He did not file for divorce but simply moved in with his new lover.

His wife was incensed at being abandoned for a younger woman and responded by filing a complaint against him in court in Kingston. She accused her husband of not only abandonment but also non-support as well.

After repeatedly petitioning the court and receiving empty promises from her husband, Elizabeth came before a judge more than a few times before the case was given its day in 1897.

Terwilliger found himself in Police Court in Kingston to answer the charges of abandonment and non-support made by his wife, Elizabeth. He denied taking up with another woman and abandoning his wife but, in the end, agreed to pay monthly support to Elizabeth. If he thought things could not get worse, he was surely mistaken.

Peter B. Markle, a woodsman, stood in a store near his home in Samsonville reading the local newspaper; he had to shake his head and reread the words in front of him. Markle stared at the writing in disbelief. There, in the newspaper, was a woman who seemed to fit the description of his wife. A Civil War veteran, Markle had enlisted in the 120th New York Volunteers on January 9, 1864, in Company B. Eventually, in early 1865, he was transferred to the Seventy-third. Once the war was over for him, Private Markle returned to his beloved home in Samsonville, where he met a woman named Elizabeth whom he quickly nicknamed Liza. The two wed in 1869. He fetched his tattered old Union uniform and forager cap to make the long journey to the courthouse in Kingston.

During Elizabeth Terwilliger's testimony, the doors to the courtroom swung open. In his disheveled uniform, Private Markle entered the courtroom. The judge asked the man to state his business, as individuals in the courtroom

Rip Van Winkle. *Courtesy of Library of Congress.*

whispered to each other about who this man who burst in to the court could possibly be. Elizabeth became uncomfortable because the man was transfixed on her as he made his way towards her. When he entered, perhaps by coincidence, Elizabeth was testifying that she had been married before but that her first husband had been killed years ago. There was one thing Markle was sure of: he was anything but dead. How he actually met his fate is not stated.

A voice bellowed from the man's throat: "Do you know me, Liza?" Elizabeth looked at the old man standing in the court aisle and managed to utter out a "no." According to the *New York Times*, Markle continued, "What! You mean to tell me you don't know your first husband, Peter B. Markle?" A moment passed as the woman he called Liza fainted. She came to only to hear the account made by Markle.

Private Markle recounted to the court that the woman he knew as Liza was his lawful wife; she had a habit of doing the same thing she was accusing her husband, Terwilliger, of doing. Liza frequently abandoned him, and by his account, she had done it several times during their marriage. Liza only returned when Markle searched for her and brought her back home to Samsonville. The last time she did this, he decided that he would not look for her anymore. He decided to leave Samsonville, like so many others, and head West. While out West wandering, he claimed to have lived with Cherokee Indians, probably in Oklahoma, where they made him a sub-chief. However, he longed for his hometown of Samsonville and eventually returned.

After hearing this turn of events, the court dismissed the case after Markle's presence proved that he was in fact alive and well. He shocked the court by telling the judge that he intended on suing Elizabeth for bigamy. It does not appear that this actually ever happened. Perhaps being exposed by the public court in Kingston and facing a possible charge of bigamy, it was to Elizabeth's advantage to reunite with her first husband and avoid further humiliation.

According to the 1900 U.S. Census, Markle was still living in the town of Rochester, where Samsonville was located, and was married to an Elizabeth. Peter and Elizabeth eventually moved to Phoenicia, according to the 1920 U.S. Census. Peter B. Markle, the Rip Van Winkle of the Catskills, died there in 1927.

CHAPTER 3

The Craft Episode

Murder in Lattingtown

In May 1909, Martin and Ellen Fallon lived in a modest house in Lattingtown, which was located in Marlborough. The Federal Census for 1900 gives us a glimpse into the life of this couple. Ellen was born in New York City, and both of her parents had immigrated to the United States. She was thirty-four years old in 1900. Her husband was a more recent transplant to New York, having only been in the United States since 1880. He lived in the Twentieth Ward of Manhattan before moving to Lattingtown. He was not a farmer, like his neighbors the Crafts, but a hotel clerk. By 1900, the Fallons had three children: Mary, Joseph and a newborn named Vincent. The forty-five-year-old Martin Fallon owned his home and had enough money to send his two older children to school. When not working, he tended the currant bushes that lined the front of his house.

The 1900 Federal Census listed Frank Craft as forty-two years old. His wife, Annie, had relatively recently celebrated her thirty-eighth birthday. The couple had two sons; one was named Henry, and his younger brother was named Leighton. They helped their father farm the 170 acres that the family owned.

The Crafts and the Fallons shared a common property line. There was a school that was located on this property line, and sometimes the Crafts, who were affluent farmers, did some work for the school or helped tend to its needs. The easiest and most direct route to the school was through the Fallon property, in order to avoid a culvert that could be tough to navigate with a team of horses.

Two men standing with the Fallon house in the background. *Courtesy of Elizabeth M. Werlau.*

According to testimony in the local papers, there was no known animosity between the two families. However, something between the families was about to change on May 28, 1909. After a brief confrontation, Fallon lay dead on the front lawn with a fatal gunshot wound; this set off a trial that captivated Ulster County and the residents of Lattingtown.

One afternoon, Craft decided to load up a flat board that he intended to pile with stone—he wanted to remove some rails at the school. The easiest way to access these rails was through the Fallon property. Craft did not feel as though he needed to ask his neighbor for the right-of-way.

The Craft home.
*Courtesy of Elizabeth
M. Werlau.*

Craft drove his horses on, and as soon as he crossed onto Fallon's property, Fallon flew out of the house and confronted him. He shouted that if he did not get off his property, he would kill both Craft and his horses. Fallon was brandishing a pair of sheep shears; thus, Craft retreated to the safety of his own property. What happened next is open to conjecture because, after another altercation, Fallon lay dead on his lawn from a bullet hole.

Craft's son Henry was in his twenties and helped his father when he was not working at the Mitchel Garage, where he held a job for around six months. According to testimony, he was a chauffeur. He heard about the commotion going on between his father and Fallon. In response, he took their team of horses and, along with a worker from the farm, decided to haul stone up to the school crossing on the Fallon property line. Why he particularly was hauling the stone is not stated in the newspapers, but he knew that he would go through the Fallon's territory. Later testimony revealed the belief that the twenty-three-year-old Craft son was forcing a confrontation with Fallon.

As soon as Henry Craft crossed onto the property, according to the worker accompanying him, the young man started calling out to Fallon and daring him to come out and do something. What no one knew, except for the elder Craft, was that his son was armed with a pistol. As expected, Fallon flew out of the house with a club, threatening the younger Craft. He was told by Henry Craft not to touch his team of horses and to put the weapon down.

Some witnesses at Henry Craft's trial reported that Fallon did hit his horses. After repeated warnings, Henry Craft finally drew his pistol and fired into the dirt three times. All witnesses agreed that the fourth shot somehow hit Fallon, who fled on to his property, where he fell to the ground. Thinking nothing of this, Henry Craft continued on with his stone to his original destination.

On the way back, a worker traveling with Henry Craft suggested that he check on Fallon. Craft realized that Fallon was dead after he told him to get up with no response; consequently, a doctor was called and arrived a short time later. After declaring Fallon deceased, the doctor performed a brief autopsy declaring that, in his opinion, the cause of Fallon's death was one bullet, which severed a major artery. Realizing the severity of the situation, Henry Craft returned home to discuss the situation with his father. They agreed that Henry Craft needed to turn himself in, which he did to Deputy Sheriff William L. DeWitt. Accompanied by DeWitt and Judge Woolsey, he was taken to Kingston, where he was placed in jail.

During the first week in June, the results of Fallon's official autopsy by county coroner Alex Hasbrouck were reported. Assistant District Attorney Traver and District Attorney Cunningham began interviewing witnesses, of which there were about six. Henry Craft was represented by Eldorous Dayton of nearby Marlborough, and later, when the case was transferred to the state Supreme Court, a second lawyer was added to the case named Augustus H. Van Buren. John B. Ball, of Milton, represented Mrs. Fallon. As the lawyers would quickly realize, the testimony of the witnesses differed substantially from that of Henry Craft and his worker.

The first witness interviewed was Robert Conn. He claimed in the *Kingston Daily Freeman* that he was not more than thirty feet away from the whole incident. In his testimony, he stated that Henry Craft drove his horses up on Fallon's sidewalk and started calling him out and threatening to shoot him if he came out of the house. He admitted to overhearing Henry Craft telling the man to keep away from his horses. However, he did not recall any threats being made by Fallon. When Fallon approached the horses, Henry Craft shot four times; by the fourth shot, Conn saw Fallon drop. Conn continued that Henry Craft then continued with his stone to the schoolhouse. When the seriousness of the situation was apparent, a doctor was finally called, but it was too late. Conn added that shortly after the shooting, Mrs. Fallon saw her husband's lifeless body and accused Henry Craft of killing her husband.

Isaac E. Conklin was the next person to be called as a witness; he was three hundred yards away when he heard the gun go off. He agreed with Conn and stated that he only heard Fallon yell when he was blasted and collapsed. He told Traver that there was little chance that Henry Craft's worker saw or heard much of what happened, as he was ahead of them during their journey.

Conklin was followed by Theron Hall, who believed he was four hundred yards away from the incident. He was a blacksmith who owned a shop a short distance away. He claimed to have seen the shooting when he looked to see what was upsetting the team of horses and causing them to rear. He related that he did see Fallon near the team and that four shots were also audible. When he looked for Fallon again, he was lying in the grass. When he rushed over to Fallon, he commented that he found a small pocketknife next to the man's body that he had subsequently handed over as evidence.

Henry Craft was eventually indicted of murder in the first degree, and his case was transferred to the state Supreme Court, where he would stand trial. George H. Fitts, of Albany, would be the justice who would preside over the criminal case. Before the trial could begin, however, a jury needed to be chosen.

The jurors were selected by December 16, 1909, with Pulaski Birch as the foreman of the jury. The trial was to begin the next day, on December 17. However, no one could have predicted what would occur next. The following morning, when Justice Fitts did not come down from his room at the Hotel Eagle for breakfast, he was found dead in his bed. It was reported that he had a heart condition, so presumably he died of a heart attack. Fitts was replaced by Judge Betts, and Betts promptly dismissed the jury and adjourned the court sine die.

Court was back in session by May 1910. The new justice presiding over the selection was not Betts, but Judge Chester. He directed that a new jury needed to be selected. Even before the actual trial started, Van Buren, the defense attorney, argued with the judge that he disagreed with a new jury being selected because there had already been one chosen in December 1909. Van Buren purported that this was the jury that should be involved with the case. He continued, according to one newspaper, that the new judge did not have the authority to dismiss the jury. Van Buren felt that such a change would place his client in jeopardy, and thus he should be tried by the first jury. His motion was denied, and the trial moved forward with John G. Meyers as the new foreman.

The federal census was conducted again in 1910. The enumerator came to the house and farm of Frank Craft, and something interesting transpired. He was listed again in the census, as was his wife, Annie, and son Leighton. The enumerator also entered Henry's name, but then it was crossed out.

Regarding Henry Craft's trial, the jury was given the case to decide by the close of the day on May 12, 1910. They reconvened and found Henry Craft guilty of murder in the second degree and not the first degree, as he was originally indicted for. He was sentenced to twenty years to life in Dannemora Prison. An almost immediate appeal was filed by the defense.

It was hoped the appeal would be heard by the fall of 1911. Meanwhile, Henry Craft remained in prison, and yet another important individual to his trial died: Dayton, the other half of his legal team. The lower court's ruling was reaffirmed and Henry Craft stayed behind bars until the summer of 1915, when, according to the *Ostego Farmer*, Governor Whitman commuted his sentence from the original twenty years to "five years, three months and three days." The reason given for this decreased jail term was "mitigating circumstances." Craft had been locked up since the murder occurred in 1909.

There is no indication that Henry Craft ever returned to Marlborough. The federal census of 1920 shows that Leighton, his brother, was married with two daughters. He is listed as a fruit farmer. His father, Frank, is also listed as living with his son and daughter-in-law. There is no mention of his mother, Annie. Joseph Fallon, the oldest son of Martin and Ellen Fallon, remained in Marlborough as a farmer according to the 1920 census.

CHAPTER 4

The Ashokan Slasher

It was billed as the worst murder in recent memory. The first capital execution in a quarter of a century, the crime itself was vicious in nature. The man at the center of the memorable historical event was a day laborer on the Ashokan; his name was Samuel Ford, a transplant from New York City.

Ford did not make headlines when he arrived in Ulster County prior to March 1909. Just like many laborers, he heard about the mammoth undertaking known as the construction of the Ashokan Reservoir in the Catskills, far to the northwest of New York City. He decided to make his way up to an employment opportunity, journeying with his wife, named Captora.

Ford arrived in High Falls in February 1909 and applied for a job to work on the aqueduct. He and his wife resided there with a family that ran a boardinghouse. Ford's employment and stay in High Falls did not last long, however, as he would be involved in two scrapes with the law.

According to newspaper sources, Ford had quite an explosive temper. Frequently, that temper was unleashed on his wife. Shortly after arriving in High Falls, the local police were called to the boardinghouse for a domestic dispute. When they arrived, they were told that Ford had viciously assaulted his wife and also threatened to kill her. Police found Mrs. Ford with two black eyes and other injuries inflicted at the hands of Ford. He was promptly arrested and served ten days for this assault, as well as for possession of a handgun.

Once released from jail, Ford returned to High Falls to gather his belongings. He located his wife, who seems to have agreed to take him back, and the two relocated a short distance away to Brown's Station where once

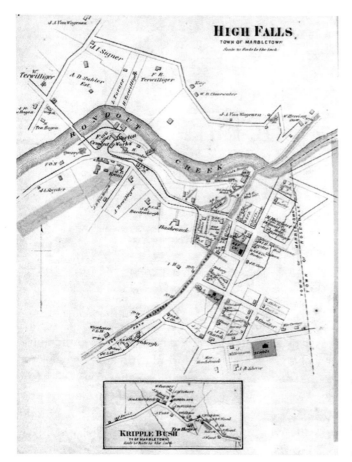

High Falls map. Today High Falls is a quaint village and a popular tourist spot. *Courtesy of Ulster County clerk's archives.*

again, he was able to secure a job working on the reservoir. It would be one of the last times Mrs. Ford would move with her husband.

In the spring of 1908, Ford was employed by MacArthur Brothers and Winston and Company, both subcontractors working for New York City on the Ashokan Reservoir. He and his wife were lodging at the house of Hugh Parish and his wife. Unfortunately, Ford could not keep it together for long, and events started to spiral out of control.

On March 27, for reasons known only to Ford, he went to his paymaster to get all of the earnings owed to him. Once paid, he made his way back to the Parish residence where he was met by his wife—she must have known he was getting paid, for she asked him for money he had promised to give to her for new clothing and shoes. Instead, she encountered a stern-faced Ford who claimed he had no money to share. Mrs. Ford became enraged as a knock came on the door: it was Mrs. Parish. She asked Ford for the current rent he owed her, as well as for back rent. He took out a dollar and asked her to put it toward the rest of his account. Mrs. Parish grew angry that the couple still could not pay their board and finally asked the deadbeat tenant and his wife to leave.

Mrs. Ford, who was at her wit's end with her husband, and also perhaps tired of his beatings, begged the Parishes to let her stay. She implored them to throw her husband out instead, but her pleadings were to no avail. The couple vacated the house with Mrs. Ford yelling at her husband that she was going to leave him and return to New York City. Later on during his trial, Ford would claim that Parish and two other men forced him out of the home at knifepoint.

The couple needed a place to stay and arrived at Pine Cunningham's boardinghouse later on that same day, March 27, 1909. The mistress of the home handed Ford a key to a room; once she was gone and he and his wife were in the room, he locked the door and refused to give Mrs. Ford the key. With no way out, she began to scream and yell, begging and pleading for him to free her. Mrs. Ford kept saying she wanted to leave him. The arguing became louder and louder until a knock came on the door. It was Mrs. Cunningham; through the door, Mrs. Ford begged her to let her out. Finally after much discussion, Ford was persuaded to open the door and give up the key.

Rosendale and D&H. *Courtesy of Library of Congress.*

This was more than Mrs. Ford could stand. Once the front door was ajar, she waited for Ford to exit and then slammed and locked the door behind him. She looked for another way of egress but found none. When she reopened the front door to run outside, she ran right into her husband, who pushed her back inside. She finally got away, heading down Brown Station Road, with her husband in pursuit close behind. About twenty minutes later, neighbors around the boardinghouse heard a bone-chilling scream from Mrs. Ford. Ford had produced a razor from his pocket and slashed his wife five times. One of the gashes was from ear to ear, almost severing her head and breaking the blade in half. As her husband walked away, she staggered into a local hospital office, where she collapsed and died.

The police found Ford not too long after the crime in Arkville, which was located about thirty miles away in Greene County. When he was searched, they found the other half of the blade they had found at the crime scene. He was sent to the Ulster County Jail in Kingston.

Ford's trial opened in September 1909, and he was convicted by the jury on September 30, 1909, of first-degree murder in the death of his wife. He denied that he killed Mrs. Ford and claimed that he did not know who committed the crime. This was despite the testimony of his deceased wife's sister, who claimed that she was told on numerous occasions by Mrs. Ford that she feared for her life. In October 1909, his appeal was taken up by the Court of Appeals in Albany, where it was rejected. Ford was sentenced to die in the electric chair during the first week of November 1909.

Before his departure to Dannemora for his execution, jailer Seth Jocelyn asked if Ford had been searched. The jailer was told that nothing was found on Ford's person. Jocelyn told Deputy Sheriff Cohen that Ford must be hiding something if they couldn't even locate the money left over from his pay. They ordered Ford to take his shoes off. Ford removed one shoe and revealed ten dollars in wages that he had claimed to his late wife not to possess. While sitting on a bed, as Ford prepared to take off his other shoe, he quickly concealed and hid a weapon in the bed. According to newspapers, it was a knife that was sharpened like a razor and could easily be opened—his plan was to stab his guards and make an escape.

Another prisoner witnessed what Ford did with the knife and reported it. As Cohen searched for the blade with his hand, he ended up cutting his fingers open. However, Cohen owed a debt of gratitude to Jocelyn, who asked that the prisoner be searched again before he left for Dannemora, which resulted in their lives being spared. Ford never learned of their discovery because he was taken directly from his cell for transport.

CHAPTER 5
Fannie Toth and a Slasher Named Robert Digs

Today, High Falls is a quaint little town located in Marbletown. It is known for its little specialty shops, restaurants and stunning falls. The town was also known for being a stop on the D&H Canal. However, with the construction of the Ashokan Reservoir and the influx of workers into the area, life in some ways started to change for the small town. This especially held true with the propagation of both licensed and unlicensed saloons, boardinghouses and eateries.

Once New York City decided it was going to build the Ashokan Reservoir, its construction was compared to the building of the Panama Canal in Central America. It was a monumental task for the time period, involving large numbers of workers and displacing many towns and villages and the people who lived in them. Many of the workers heading north were immigrants from New York City hoping to find well-paying and long-term work. Many of them were upstanding individuals, but there were a number of them who were less than desirable.

The arrival of thousands of workers sometimes created problems for the communities that were in proximity to the construction of the Ashokan. One locality hit hard by the emergence of work camps around the areas was High Falls. One of the aqueduct's shafts, called Shaft Number Five, was identified in local papers as a particular nuisance area. Yet another troublesome spot was known as Pistol Row, known for the proliferation of handguns there. It was considered to be one of the more dangerous parts of High Falls.

Canal locks at High Falls. Some of these locks can be seen today. *Author's collection.*

Because the workers often had idle time and indulged in alcohol and, to a lesser extent, cocaine, crime seemed to be on the rise around town. One of the constant situations that needed to be addressed by law enforcement was the high rate of violence that often resulted from alcohol use. Thus, a special police force was created specifically to deal with the disruptions caused to the area by the mammoth construction project.

There was a police force that was stationed in High Falls, as well as in other areas surrounding the reservoir project, in order to keep an eye on, and ultimately keep in check, the thousands of workers that were streaming into the area. Sometimes referred to as the Plumland Police, which was then considered to be a derogatory name, the proper name for this law force was the Board of Water Supply Police. It became the board's job to ensure that workers were not carrying weapons and were respecting the local towns that they were near. The workers were mostly under its jurisdiction, leaving the local authorities to deal with native citizens.

The workers' antics were only part of the problem. Another segment of the equation was the relocation of people into the area who sought to profit underhandedly from the workers. Many of these individuals did not obtain licenses, and once they were busted or closed up by the Water Supply Police, they would simply open up in another locale. When an establishment was licensed, the police could raid the business and look for weapons and/or at least restrict the hours in which the workers could be there or in town. These situations became cat-and-mouse games.

One of the disruptive individuals alluded to above was Fannie Toth. The results of her case are less important than the problems wayward people like her caused for the community. Toth was not from High Falls, but she lived a short distance away in Kingston. Specifically, she lived in East Kingston, where she ran a boardinghouse; prior to that, she was the caretaker of another boardinghouse northeast of Kingston in Hudson.

Once she arrived in High Falls, Toth promptly opened up a place for workers to eat near Shaft Number Five. In October 1908, the *Kingston Daily Freeman* reported that the name of her establishment was the Blind Tiger. It was written that she did not run a boardinghouse here, as she did not have enough room to provide board. She sometimes employed her nephew to wait tables.

The Water Supply Police started to hear reports about this eatery illegally serving alcohol to reservoir workers and became determined to put it out of business. They created a sting operation involving two officers, including an officer named Auckner. The policemen posed as workers from the shaft and ordered beer. Toth's nephew quickly served them. Auckner and the other officer consumed eight bottles of beer, which became an issue later, and after paying for them arrested Toth. According to a newspaper report, when the lawmen identified themselves, Toth was quite shocked to see the officers and even more surprised that they were served beer—she claimed that she was at a loss as to where that beer came from in the first place.

Once in custody, Toth was hauled before a justice of the peace in High Falls and was subsequently sent to the Ulster County Jail in Kingston, which was located in the courthouse. When the examination of evidence commenced on October 2, 1908, Toth's lawyer asked that the charges be dismissed because he felt his client was held without being charged. He further contended that the excise tax law that Toth allegedly violated did not apply to her. The prosecutor argued successfully that the law had in fact been changed and that Toth was charged properly and thus did breach the excise tax law. The judge agreed and threw out the motion for dismissal; furthermore, he ordered that Toth be held until October 7. The justice of the peace also ordered bail to be set at $1,000.

Some of Toth's friends attempted to raise the bail money, but they were unable to do so and she was thus held in jail in Kingston. The case is unusual because water supply officers were frequently frustrated that local court systems did not always collaborate with them; sometimes, they released individuals like Toth with nothing more than a slap on the wrist. Clearly, that was not the case this time.

The sting operation was meant to curb alcohol abuse and the problems that went along with it. Individuals with little else to do would drink their wages away, and when they no longer had money to support their drinking habits, they were known to rob the citizens in towns like High Falls that were near their camps. At that time, newspapers were chock full of stories of incidences of burglary and other forms of wickedness around the camps.

An example of the types of crimes that occurred around High Falls occurred when a man was robbed on Mountain Road the same year that the police arrested Toth. Once the man handed over his twenty-eight cents to the criminals, which is all that he had on him, they let him go. Another man was robbed of ten dollars and yet another of a silver watch. Frequently, the robbers just wanted beer money, and they made that known to their prey. Once the cash or valuables were handed over, they let the person go.

A prime example of an excessively drunken troublemaker was Robert Digs; he was a frequent visitor to the Jackson Saloon in High Falls, which was also located near Shaft Five. Digs, who was in his mid-twenties, was originally from Newport News, Virginia. He left his wife behind and came to High Falls, like so many other individuals, in order to find employment associated with the construction the Ashokan.

One evening in September 1909, Digs had just been paid for work as a laborer when he decided to head over to the Jackson Saloon. According to Jackson, the owner of the bar, Digs entered the saloon and produced a ten dollar bill to buy drinks for the other patrons. A harbinger of things to come, Digs began to argue with the owner, who was also tending the bar. When given back his change, Digs accused the barkeep of short-changing him. Digs then seemed to have either realized his mistake or became distracted by a Nannie Davis, who lived nearby on Pistol Row.

Digs began to talk to the young lady and might have even considered her his date for the night. Witnesses in the saloon paid no mind to the two when they were talking or even when they went outside. Shortly after accompanying Digs outside, Davis came back in with her dress ripped and screamed, "Help me!"

According to Digs, the problem between the two erupted over money. He claimed that when he took out what he thought was a dollar to give to the woman, he realized that it was a five dollar bill. Digs claimed that she grabbed the money from his hand and then ran inside, exclaiming that she wanted a gun to shoot him with. Claiming that he feared for his life, he took out a razor and slashed her violently; one gash was so deep that it was only stopped by her rib cage. The woman was taken to the hospital, where she was treated and remained for ten days. It was noted that after she left the hospital, she lived with the owner of the saloon, even though he was married but did not live with his wife or kids.

Those who witnessed the above events unfold told a story that differed from Digs's. It was claimed that Davis was the one who was by the door holding a dollar bill in her hand. According to a paper reporting on the story, Digs took her dollar, and she began to yell at him for doing so. He then became irate and grabbed Davis, tearing her dress. According to testimony, he said that he would kill his mother for money.

Davis was able to get away and back into the saloon, where she asked for help. After a period of time when she thought things had settled down and that Digs had left, she started for home. Digs did not leave but was actually waiting in the shadows for Davis. Once she was outside, he attacked her with his razor. After the slashing, Digs took off; a short time later, he was apprehended.

When Digs was brought to trial, the jury and Judge Cantine believed the story of the witnesses and Davis. Digs was convicted in October and sent to prison at Dannemora for a term of five years. It is not known what happened to Digs or Davis. As for the Jackson Saloon, one paper reported that it had closed down.

CHAPTER 6

The Shawangunk Gang and the Lyman Freer Gang

Today, people look up at the Shawangunk Mountains with a sense of awe and respect. However, there was a time when people viewed the Shawangunks as a haven for the wicked of Ulster County. These beautiful rugged mountains were sometimes used as a sanctuary or hideout for unsavory characters, such as the Shawangunk Gang. According to newspapers ranging from the *New York Times* to the *Kingston Daily Freeman*, armed men were quite a nuisance in these areas from the late 1870s to 1881. Two of these more famous individuals were Lyman Freer and, still later, Big Bad Bill Monroe.

These outlaws and other individuals like them were hard to bring to justice because they hid in the most remote areas of the mountains; oftentimes, victims were afraid of pursuing them. Many had long-standing ties in those mountains, with family members who were all too happy to protect their kin, by force if necessary, as some lawmen found out. It was believed that these unsavory characters were hailing from settlements of Logtown, near Accord, or Stony Kill on the western-facing slopes of the Shawangunks.

These desperadoes stole anything that they could get their hands on; it appears that no target was too small. What they stole ranged from chickens to butter. One newspaper noted that they sometimes stole horse teams in order to cart away their other pilfered goods. Once this task was complete, they frequently abandoned the horses.

Though some of these gangs had their home bases in Ulster County, they did not limit themselves to just preying on towns in this area. They also roamed the small towns and villages of neighboring Sullivan and Orange

Road in the Gunks. Crisscrossing the property are miles of carriage trails that guests used for horse and carriage rides. Today, many overnight and day guests use them for hiking. *Courtesy of Library of Congress.*

Counties as well. They were not always satisfied with just targeting farmers or businesses. Because, in many cases, towns and villages refused to pursue these gangs, the marauders were emboldened and upped the ante by also targeting railroads and post offices. This would prove to be a fatal flaw.

It seems that one particular group of renegades crossed the line when they started robbing both railroad depots and post offices. Some of these centers were located in Shawangunk, Thompson Ridge, Summitville and Phillipsport. The *New York Times* believed that the same group of men was involved in a counterfeit money operation running out of Sullivan and Orange Counties, which increasingly gained the attention of both state and local officials.

Even guests traveling up to Lake Mohonk were not immune to these troublemakers. A group of three highway men attempted, on at least two different occasions, to rob guests of Albert K. Smiley, the owner of the Mohonk Mountain House, at gunpoint. Mr. Smiley responded by offering a

$100 reward for their capture, but the men faded into the rugged mountains. It is believed they were never brought to justice.

Many outlaws over the years were instrumental in their own undoing because they became too confident and simply talked too much at the wrong time—and the Shawangunk Gang was no exception. The gang's undoing, as written in the *New York Times*, was due in part to a conversation someone had overheard while at the home of Anthony Baker, believed to be a principal ringleader of one of the gangs. One of his own relatives relayed what he had heard there about an earlier robbery of one of Baker's neighbors, which involved the gang. He had also overheard two men discussing a relatively recent robbery of the Wallkill Valley Railroad Company Station, which had been robbed twice, as well as the burglary of a milk house of a wealthy farmer who lived at the base of the mountains. One of these two men was Baker, who was fifty-five years old and relatively affluent.

It was thought that Baker's recent migration from the area around Accord had something to do with the recent crime wave within neighboring territories. It was also believed by many that his home was the headquarters for the Shawangunk Gang. Other key gang leaders were Garrett S. Smith, George A. Smith and John B. Mercile. The last man also caught the eye of a stationmaster, Mr. Bostwick, whose station had been recently robbed. Bostwick believed that recent robberies coincided with the arrival of the thirty-year-old Mercile. According to the man who stumbled upon a meeting at Baker's home, this gang was thought to be numbered at around thirteen individuals.

Bostwick decided to take a stand against the Shawangunk Gang. As mentioned, his station had been robbed twice in two years. He started to take notice of a gang of young men that frequented the town and were quite rowdy. Equally of interest was that they frequented taverns; though they had no visible sign of employment, they never seemed to lack money or finer things.

A warrant was secured from Justice Frank K. Hasbrouck to search the homes of Baker and Garrett S. Smith. It was agreed that the best man for the job was the forty-year-old Shawangunk constable, Jo Millspaugh. Millspaugh's first stop was Smith's house, where stolen goods from recent robberies were found. After Smith's house, the constable, along with another officer, searched Baker's home and found additional items that had been reported missing.

According to an account from a New York City newspaper, Baker became very suspicious that Mercile happened to show up while his home was being searched. It was his feeling that Mercile was talking to the authorities in an effort to save his own skin. While the house was being investigated by officers, the two men stepped behind an outbuilding to discuss Baker's feelings towards Mercile. Unbeknownst to them, they were being listened to by one of the officers searching the home. Once the search was finished, the officer, who had heard the conversation between the two men in which they admitted to their acts of thievery, secured an arrest warrant for both of the Smiths and Mercile on October 7, 1881.

The local constable was sent to arrest Mercile, who lived in an area of the mountains called the Trapps; unfortunately, however, he was not at home. It was decided that he might be at the home of Garrett S. Smith. Once the constable arrived, he told an officer accompanying him to go around to the back of Smith's dwelling. When he knocked at the door, he was told by Mrs. Smith that he could not enter. Hearing a commotion from within the house, the constable responded to Mrs. Smith's refusal by kicking in the door.

Once through the door, Mercile, who had been hiding in the home, fired at the constable and struck him just below the shoulder. The wounded Millspaugh called out to his partner that he had been shot. Mercile fled out of the door, firing a few more times at the officer and also at the injured Millspaugh. The pursuit continued until Mercile fell over a fence, with the constable landing on top of him. The two men struggled as Mercile found his pistol, leveled it at point-blank range and fired directly at the forehead of the lawman. Constable Millspaugh screamed for his partner, who jumped on Mercile before he could fire a second time at Millspaugh. Remarkably, Millspaugh was able to assist with handcuffing Mercile.

When the two lawmen arrived in town, there was considerable commotion as Justice Hasbrouck's presence was requested in order to start the wheels of justice in motion. While this was going on, the wounded Millspaugh went to the local doctor for treatment. Word quickly spread about what had happened to the popular constable; in response, a crowd formed around the local hotel and cried out for Mercile to be dragged out and lynched. Cooler heads prevailed, as Hasbrouck arrived for the hearing. Justice Hasbrouck, in turn, called District Attorney Clearwater to come to Shawangunk as quickly as possible. Eventually both Smiths and Mercile were sent to Kingston to be held in jail until November, when their case would be heard before a grand jury. Baker was sent to the Albany jail for ninety days.

In the end, both Smiths and Mercile were sentenced to five years in the Clinton State Prison at Dannemora. All of the men were sentenced to hard labor. The constable who had been shot by Mercile eventually recovered and returned to his duties.

The demise of the Shawangunk Gang allowed the farmers of the area to breathe a collective sigh of relief. However, as one gang was eliminated, a new one rose to prominence. At times, this gang also used the Shawangunks as a hideout and operated in much the same area as the Shawangunk Gang. There was an exception, however; this gang also lifted goods from areas as far away as Danbury in neighboring Connecticut.

At just about the same time that the Shawangunk Gang's leaders were being sent to prison, a new menacing boss surfaced. Lyman Freer struck fear in the populace of not only Ulster and Sullivan Counties but also in Danbury. He was the lone leader of the gang that bore his name: the Lyman Freer Gang. Members of this gang were not only known for their thievery, but they also had an equal reputation for their generous use of violence against anyone who stood in their way.

This gang had such a terrifying reputation for violence that many law officers did not want to tangle with them. Some of the horrific acts they performed included robbing people on roads, stealing wagons and breaking into barns—they basically stole anything that was not nailed down to the ground. As with the Shawangunk Gang, many local citizens decided that it was best for them to just look the other way. If someone tried to take a stand against this gang, he could find his home burned or, even worse, he could turn up dead.

There was one brave individual, however, who was not afraid to take on the Lyman Freer Gang. He just needed a solid enough lead or a witness to come forward with information about the gang or recent robberies. The gentleman who was not intimidated by this bunch of bandits was an Ulster County sheriff dubbed "Fearless" Phil Schantz by those who knew him and his work.

Schantz was the Ulster County sheriff from 1895 to 1897, and it was during this time period that he was dubbed "Fearless." This nickname was given, in part, because he was not afraid to go after the worst criminals. Even the criminals knew that once he was on your trail, he usually caught up with you and brought you to justice. His fearlessness was exalted in the papers of the day. One such example, that was the subject of a newspaper article, involved the murder of William Gardner at the hands of Joseph Decker. This murder occurred in Plattekill.

After the murder, Decker became a fugitive and frequently moved from place to place to avoid the law. A large reward amounting to $500 had been placed on his head and posted by at least three police departments in and around Plattekill. He was known to be armed and dangerous.

One afternoon, Schantz was on a drive with his wife when he saw a man walking along the side of the road. He recognized the man from the wanted posters circulating in his office. The Ulster County sheriff realized that it was

Decker, who was just strolling along in the broad daylight. In hopes of not arousing suspicion in Decker, Schantz continued on down the road to the first house he saw and pulled into the corresponding driveway. Schantz probably identified himself and asked the owner of the house to look after his wife, as he had some police business to attend to in the area. He then went back to where he saw Decker sauntering along the side of the road. The unarmed Ulster County sheriff apprehended Decker without a struggle and then took the man to jail all by himself. The *Kingston Daily Freeman* related proudly in an article that "Fearless Phil" did not delegate the responsibility of capturing dangerous outlaws to his deputies but rather took care of these jobs himself most of the time.

It was no surprise to anyone that when word got out that the Lyman Freer Gang had struck again, this time stealing an entire team of horses in Plattekill, Schantz would pursue them. The sheriff seemed to know that they were heading to Danbury, Connecticut, where the horses would most likely be sold. Schantz also headed to Danbury, to track down the leader of the gang, and hopefully send him to jail where he belonged.

In 1896, the police in Danbury were tipped off by a telegram from the Anti-Horse Stealing Society that Freer had once again recently stolen some horses, and it was thought that he might try to sell them in Danbury. When the police investigated, they found that this tip was correct. They found the team of horses, though according to the newspapers of that time, their manes and tails had been shaved in order to make it more difficult to recognize them. An officer who trailed Freer from Ulster County, probably Schantz, confirmed that he recognized one of the horses. Freer stole not only a sorrel horse, according to the *New Haven Register*, but also a grey horse as well, and knowing these specific horses helped them hunt the team down. A closer investigation found that the horses were not all that Freer and his gang had stolen; they had also lifted a platform truck. When he was arrested, Freer also possessed a wagon that was filled with everything from carpenters tools to illustrated bibles to furniture, as well as horse harnesses.

Schantz brought the era of the Lyman Freer Gang to a close in 1896 when he arrested Freer in Danbury. Freer had one desperate act left in him before he was escorted back to Ulster County to stand trial. He reached into his pocket and produced a large roll of bills, no doubt his profit from fencing stolen goods, and peeled off a $100 bill, telling the arresting officer that if he looked the other way, the money would be his. Freer's offer was in vain.

Once in Ulster County, Freer stood trial. He was sentenced to seven years, to be served in Dannemora Prison. The era of lawlessness that had locals on edge was rapidly coming to an end.

CHAPTER 7

Big Bad Bill Monroe

The Gardiner Desperado

Route 208 meanders from Main Street in the village of New Paltz through new subdivisions and old farms. It continues its journey to a junction with 44/55 where you find yourself in the heart of what is known as Ireland Corners in Gardiner, New York. Perhaps one of the most colorful individuals in this area's history, William Monroe, also known as "Big Bad" Bill" Monroe, called this place his home.

Monroe's name does not conjure up many memories these days. Even if you throw out his nicknames to locals—Big Bad Bill or even the Gardiner Desperado—for the most part, you get blank looks in return. About a century ago, however, this would not have been the case. At that time, residents of Ulster County hung on the exploits of this bandit, who often retreated to the rugged safety of the Shawangunk Mountains.

According to the *New York Times*, by all accounts, Monroe was a very bad man. When he made news in the summer of 1908, he was already a well-known figure to local law enforcement officials. When he assaulted not only one member of the Deyo family, but all six members, as well as their farm workers, not too many people were surprised. Twice wounded, pursued through two states by farmers and dogs, Monroe was captured as many times but managed to escape.

Ulster County citizens bought the papers every day to hear about Monroe's latest exploits. In short, he became something of a legend. Fact began to blend with fiction as rumors spread that he openly mocked the long arm of the law and at one point offered a bounty on his own head.

"Big Bad Bill." A court drawing and the one known image of the "Bad Man." *Courtesy of the* Kingston Daily Freeman.

The outlaw named the time and place where he would be, daring anyone to capture him, as will be detailed later in this story.

According to the *Kingston Daily Freeman*, Monroe liked his drink. When he drank too much, he became rowdy and prone to fighting. One day, he appeared at the Deyo homestead in Ireland Corners in Gardiner. Some accounts state that he wanted to work but was refused the chance; others assert that he wanted to rent a house that belonged to the Deyos. Both accounts agree that Abram Deyo told Monroe something he did not want to hear, thus causing him to fly off the handle. When he was rejected by Deyo, who lived at the homestead with his family, the 155-pound Monroe swung immediately at Deyo and knocked him out cold, laying claim to his reputation. Once down, Monroe continued to assault Deyo until others tried to intervene.

Someone ran to get Deyo's brother Jonathan for help. Jonathan was a lawyer from New York City who was visiting with his family. Jonathan entered the barn only to be attacked by Monroe with an iron bar. Monroe fled the barn and entered the Deyo house, assaulting both men's wives and their children. He left the home and turned his attention to the barn; after assaulting the farmhands there, he burned it to the ground. A newspaper wrote that he cut all of the phone lines just before he fled back to Jenkinstown, where he lived.

After the effects of the alcohol wore off, Monroe sat on his porch. He realized that the authorities would soon come for him. He decided that his plan would be to take off for the mountains to meet up with other bad seeds from the Shawangunk Gang. Monroe eluded capture, even after the town board of Gardiner posted a $100 reward for the seizure of the twenty-five-year-old. Sheriff Boice of Ulster County also offered a reward of $300 for catching Monroe. A reward poster described him as 5'6" with light hair, a stout build, a fair complexion, a tattoo of a star on his wrist and a mole on his left cheek.

Shortly after the attack on the Deyo family, Monroe was chased some one hundred miles. The local police believed, according to a paper of the day, that Monroe was heading to New Jersey, where he had some kin. Ulster County Police alerted the sheriff's department in Orange County, and off went Sheriff A.L. Decker, along with Undersheriff Frank C. Hock and a deputy sheriff named William Leonard. When they finally arrived at the home of the man they believed was a close relative of Monroe's, they approached it slowly, calling out for him to come out with his hands up.

All of a sudden, Monroe burst through the backdoor and fled toward the adjoining cornfields. In hot pursuit was Leonard, who eventually caught up with the Gardiner Desperado. Leonard drew his pistol, ordering Monroe to start walking back to the other law officers. In an instant, the outlaw pushed the deputy sheriff's gun away and bolted back into the cornfields but not before being shot several times; he fell to the ground once but picked himself back up and disappeared into a swamp. He continued to run as the blood streamed from his wounds. The officers believed that they would catch up to him when he eventually died of his wounds.

The newspapers of the era, including the *New York Times*, seemed captivated by the antics of this outlaw and members of the Shawangunk Gang. His exploits had all of the makings of a modern-day soap opera. Monroe was all too happy to oblige with more episodes for the local newspapers. Shortly after the episode with Leonard, Monroe's unpredictable nature became fodder for more stories because of a letter that he wrote to his wife. The letter was found by an individual who made it known to the public.

In his letter, Monroe wrote that the extent of his injuries surely meant death. The authorities did not believe it for a moment, especially since Monroe contradicted himself the next day by asking how he could give himself up when he was supposed to have been dead for a week. The newspaper continued that "it is a favorite past time of the Monroe-Turner-William crowd to report

Deyo House aerial, Ireland Corners, which more or less looks the same. One of the last barns, possibly the rebuild of one that burned, also met the same fate as the one that burned a number of years ago. *Courtesy of Mr. and Mrs. Dourdis.*

the death of members who are wanted for crimes." However, the problem was that they often overdid the letters, making them unbelievable.

The Monroe-Turner-William reference was to the family of Monroe. He was one of thirteen children born to William Monroe Sr., who was originally from Putnam County. His mother was a Turner, a notorious family that one paper said lived in and around the Shawangunk, Gardiner and New Paltz areas. They were known for terrorizing their communities and intimidating individuals wishing to bring any of them to justice. One example cited was the time that Big Bad Bill Monroe asked a local farmer in Gardiner if he could rent a cabin on his property. The farmer refused only to find his cabin burned to the ground shortly after refusing the renter. This is a possible reason that law enforcement was not keen to apprehend the Gardiner madman.

One Gardiner resident was not intimidated by the family's reputation. He spoke to a reporter for a local paper and gave advice on how to deal effectively with them: "There is only one way to deal with that crowd, and that is to get the drop on them first and blaze away. If you don't happen to have a gun, use a pitchfork, and if that isn't handy, take a club or a rock."

The resident went on to say that it was time that the community dealt with these families and put them in their places. The community had tolerated them for long enough. The same time that this article was written, Katie Monroe, the wife of Bill, was released from the county jail. She was kept to prevent her from joining her husband and also as possible bait for his return. When it became apparent that he was not reappearing, they let her return to Jenkinstown.

Readers of the *New York Times* were amused when they read in September 1908 that the Gardiner badman taunted law enforcement officials by pinning a notice to a tree a few days before the Orange County Fair. The notice told authorities, or anyone else, that he would be present at the Orange County Fair; the notice also offered a $500 award for his own capture. Newspapers reported that he did show up at his designated place. When called a liar by those who came hunting for him to collect the reward for his capture, Monroe responded that he was indeed there; however, he was dressed up as a poor widow. The paper reported that just before making his escape, he let a few people know who he was, and then he was gone again.

Deputy Sheriff Cohen trailed Monroe through Orange County, Sullivan County and even New Jersey; all of his efforts were futile. However, every week in the papers there was a sighting of Monroe with a belief that his next meal would be in prison, for even he could not elude capture forever. It all came to an end when a sheriff contacted authorities in Ulster County, informing them that he had in fact located their "perp" in an unlikely location.

Big Bad Bill managed to remain on the loose for some sixteen months, until November 1909, when law enforcement in California alerted the Ulster County Sheriff's Department that they had arrested Monroe for theft. It was believed by that time that he might have headed out west to stay with his sister who lived in Bakersfield, California. Ulster County Sheriff Boice filed extradition papers and, along with Orange County Sheriff Decker, headed west, taking a train to El Centra, California, where Monroe was being held.

Newspapers throughout this period continued to follow Big Bad Bill's escapades, from the time of the assault in 1908 until his apprehension in 1909. Once the two sheriffs returned to Ulster County near Christmas 1909 with their charge, newspapers again covered the story with sensational headlines. According to the papers of the day, Monroe enjoyed the notoriety, stating at one point that he was glad to be home in Ulster County where the jails were nicer than in California. He continued that he did not like

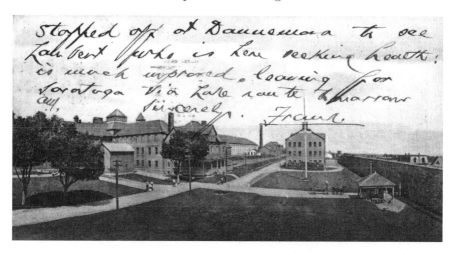

Dannemora Prison, as it is called by most, is really called Clinton Correctional Facility. *Author's collection.*

California and was especially glad that Boice came to get him. In fact, he praised both captors and stated to the press that they were fine men! Bill even said that he would not mind traveling the world with Decker and Boice. He continued that he was glad that John Lyons has not been sent because then he would have had to escape because he did not like that lawman.

Monroe felt quite like a celebrity. He was excited about the amount of guests and gawkers he would receive in jail. A news reporter covering the return of Monroe remarked that he brushed his hair, washed himself clean and even put on a new collar for the visitors that showed up to see the bad man who was on the run for sixteen months.

Upon reflection, the Gardiner Desperado's only regret was that he wished that he could have waited to return to Ulster County during his favorite time there, the spring, as opposed to during the winter. Once in jail in Ulster County, the outlaw insisted on primping himself for the public he knew would surely visit him in his jail. His antics continued as he moved closer to his trial date. The public continued to follow Big Bad Bill, even when Deputy Sherriff Cohen escorted him to the dentist for a toothache (which resulted in a root canal).

After the trial, Big Bad Bill was convicted of assaulting Jonathan Deyo in the second degree and was also convicted for assaulting other members of the Deyo family. He was sentenced to four years and eight months in jail and was sent to Dannemora Prison in Upstate New York, where, according to newspapers, he continued to create trouble by instigating riots among the

Sing-Sing Prison cell. The gunmen would have been in a cell similar to this one. *Courtesy of Library of Congress.*

inmates. In March 1910, he tried to escape and almost killed a guard in the process. This was not his only escape attempt.

Once again, Monroe tried to escape in May 1910 when he was being brought to Kingston to testify in a trial. According to local accounts, Monroe asked his handlers to use the bathroom. The two officers heard the sound of shattering glass and rushed to the bathroom only to find that he had jumped out of the bathroom window. He led the officers on a wild-goose chase through the streets of Albany. Once Monroe was caught, he begged the officers who were guarding him to kill him because he had tried to escape and told them that he would continue trying until they shot him.

Shortly after this incident, Monroe was shipped to the most notorious prison of the time, Sing-Sing, where he applied for parole in 1912. Monroe continued his exploits there as well and thus was eventually shipped back to Dannemora in

Kingston Court House. *Author's collection.*

Sing-Sing Prison, a notorious hellhole. *Courtesy of Library of Congress.*

Inside a cell at Sing-Sing. "Big Bad Bill" would have known a cell like this quite well. *Courtesy of Library of Congress.*

July 1912 (once Dannemora restored the disorder he had originally created). The warden of Sing-Sing was all too happy to see him go back from whence he came.

Once out of jail for the assaults he had committed, Monroe could not stay out of trouble for long. He made the news once again when, along with Edward Barrett, he was convicted for the brutal killing of Edward's brother Andrew. Andrew had lived in a shack on the estate of Countess d'Ivry. Monroe was eventually apprehended in New Jersey and tried in Poughkeepsie. The murder was noted for its brutality. Monroe had not only bound and tied Andrew but also hit him so violently with an axe that he almost severed the man's head. This crime was in part because of a problem the two brothers had with each other, as well as the large sums of cash that Andrew was known to keep in his residence. Monroe was sentenced to twenty years for second-degree murder.

Monroe made news one last time when he was serving his life sentence at Sing-Sing Prison in Ossining, New York. In 1925, he reported in a letter that he was not guilty of murdering Andrew Barrett and that he had a signed confession from the man who did kill him. His excuse for pleading guilty was to receive the lesser charge of second-degree murder, which did not carry the death penalty with it. There is no indication that he was ever released from prison again. As with many notable stories and individuals, the public eventually lost interest in the once notorious antics of Big Bad Bill Monroe, and he drifted into obscurity.

CHAPTER 8

It is Your Money or Your Life

In 1869, according to the book *Mohonk: Its People and Spirit*, Albert K. Smiley purchased some three hundred acres from John F. Stokes, which included a tavern that would be the basis for the Mohonk Mountain House we view today. Albert and his twin brother, Alfred, had a vision of a Quaker retreat nestled in the beautiful Shawangunk Mountains on the shore of a stunning lake called Lake Mohonk. They went to work in earnest, and by the following year in 1870, the mountain house opened up for its first season. In that same year, the Old Stage Road was built, which was "the first in a series of new carriage roads constructed between 1870 and 1910."

The mountain house also expanded in 1870; trails were established for hiking, as well as carriage trails for guests to use in order to view the stunning vistas that had drawn the twin brothers to the site. Mohonk was one of the earliest places to have indoor plumbing. It catered to individuals from New York City, as well as the well-to-do from as far away as Poughkeepsie. The last thing that guests of the Smileys' wanted was to worry about highwaymen or the Shawangunk Gang. When most people think of Mohonk Mountain House in New Paltz, they think of serenity, hiking trails, a beautiful lake, afternoon tea and wonderful views. Smiley would agree—it was the last place he wanted anyone to associate with crime or robbery. However, his worst fear became a reality in early September 1895.

Early on September 12, 1895, a group of travelers embarked from Poughkeepsie headed to their final destination of Lake Mohonk, high up in the Shawangunk Mountains outside of New Paltz. They made the long

Mohonk today consists of thousands of acres and is still owned by the Smiley Family. *Courtesy of Library of Congress.*

trip from New Paltz up into what the locals called the "Gunks." The group was filled with excitement at the prospect of a restful and exciting time at the resort and hotel. Their driver for the ride to the mountaintop resort was a man identified in the *Kingston Daily Freeman* as John Elghmie; he knew the trails to the mountain house well. As they meandered along to the resort, the group had no way of knowing that their day would become one to remember.

The group arrived at Mohonk during the afternoon of the twelfth and was most likely met by Smiley, who made a point of knowing everyone's name. He would have greeted them and welcomed them to a restful stay at his mountain retreat. After settling in, several of the young men from the party decided that they wanted to go ahead and explore an area then known as the Devil's Workshop; this was a rocky house (cave) popular with visitors to Mohonk. The men made their way on what felt like a journey toward their destination. They were enjoying their day, but unbeknownst to them, they were being watched by three individuals who aimed to do them harm. These three men were obviously not there to explore the Devil's Workshop. After they sized up their quarry, a signal was given by the leader to make their move.

Alfred K. Smiley, one of the twins who founded Mohonk Mountain House. He was a teacher before he purchased property on Lake Mohonk. *Author's collection.*

Before the group could realize what was happening, the three men were on them. One of the highwaymen pointed a gun at the chest of one of the younger individuals in the hiking party. He threatened to kill him if the others did not hand over all of their money.

The Mohonk guests fumbled through their pockets, assuring the gunman that they did not have any money on them; after all, who takes money with them when they are hiking in the woods? According to the *Kingston Daily Freeman*, after affirming that they were penniless, the gunman ordered all three tourists to run from the cave as quickly as their feet could carry them and not to look back. When one of the hikers gathered up the courage to look back, the robbers had disappeared back into the rocks.

When the young tourists returned to the hotel, they told Mohonk staff what had transpired on their way to the cave. A search party was formed at once to scour the area for the robbers but to no avail—they were not found. Looking for these individuals in the rough terrain was tantamount to searching for a needle in a haystack. The mountains were legendary as

The Shawangunks, or the Gunks, as the locals call them, can be a forbidding place even today. *Courtesy of Library of Congress.*

Mohonk Mountain House, sometimes called Lake Mohonk because of the beautiful lake that it sits on. The Mountain House was owned by the Stokes family before it was bought by the Smiley brothers. It was operated as a tavern by the Stokes family. *Courtesy of Library of Congress HABS/HAER.*

hideaways for thieves, and even before that, legend had it that the local Native Americans used the mountains as their stronghold. The mountains are chock-full of caves and sometimes almost inaccessible rocky outcrops.

When word reached Smiley about the attempted robbery of his guests, it would be an understatement to say that he was not happy about the incident. He might have looked at it as a disturbing, but isolated, occurrence. He reasoned that families and friends came to the mountaintop resort to bathe in its restful atmosphere and enjoy themselves, not get held up at gunpoint on resort property. To say the least, it was also not good for business if these robbers made a habit of sticking up guests and word of this mischief got out. Much to Smiley's dismay, this was not the last incident. It is not clear exactly when the next criminal instance transpired, but it was near the same spot where the young hikers were held up at gunpoint.

If you have ever been to the Mohonk Mountain House, it has a certain romantic allure. Even today many couples become engaged in its shadows or plan weddings amid nature's gorgeous backdrops. Perhaps feeling the same spark so many couples encounter at Mohonk, a young gentleman asked a lady to accompany him on a stroll toward the Devil's Workshop in order to enjoy the surrounding scenery. Maybe he was courting her and hoped that the two might converse.

As the couple approached some bushes, it is believed that the same three gunmen jumped out from behind them. Once again, one of the robbers pointed a gun at the gentleman's chest and threatened both him and his companion with death if they did not produce some money, and quickly at that. This time, there was no fumbling for money or pleas. Their attempt, again, unraveled as the gentleman being held at gunpoint screamed for help. Frightened by the alarm, the robbers fled the area and once again disappeared in the wilds of the Gunks.

In Smiley's mind, this was no longer a remote incident. The perpetrators of these heinous acts toward his guests had to be caught and hopefully brought to justice. Smiley promptly offered a reward of $100 for the apprehension of these menacing men or information leading to their arrest.

Where exactly these two robberies transpired is not made clear by the *Freeman* article. After numerous inquiries, and even after looking at old maps of the Mohonk Property over the years, I have tried to ascertain the approximate location of the Devil's Workshop. If it was in fact an actual destination at one point, it seems to have been lost to time or maybe a mistake made by the reporter recording the story for the newspaper. Perhaps the events that occurred at the popular landmark were not at the Devil's

Workshop but instead at the still-popular destination, the Giant's Workshop; when speaking to the reporter for the paper, someone might have nicknamed it the Devil's Workshop because of the above events.

As far as the "highway robbers," there is no compelling evidence that the three gunmen who held up two separate sets of guests in September 1895 were ever brought to justice. These incidents did not seem to be a deterrent to guests journeying to the mountaintop retreat. Instead, they faded into the rich history of Lake Mohonk.

CHAPTER 9

The Day Mohonk Almost Burned

There have been many fires in the Shawangunk Mountains in Ulster County. It is part of their ecology. In order for a vital ecosystem to exist, there must be periodic burns. The pitch pines that are unique to the Shawangunks cannot reproduce without fire. Some of these fires are started naturally by the heat of the sun, by lightning or, in some cases, by people. For example, burns were ignited by berry pickers who knew that in order to be guaranteed crops of huckleberries, the mountains had to be cleared so that the berry bushes would not be squeezed out. Sometimes these fires grew out of control and threatened the villages scattered about in the Shawangunks and at their base. One such fire occurred in May 1906.

No one was quite sure how this fire started, but it quickly grew to consume some five thousand acres. When fires like that raged, everybody was mobilized to fight them. During the 1906 fire, Fire Warden Fluckiger of Kerhonkson battled the forest fire alongside residents in order to prevent it from consuming the tiny settlement of Kerhonkson. At some points, this vast fire blocked out the sun, thus making it appear as though it was evening. In the case of this next story, the forest fire was not set off for economic benefit or by lightning: it was torched.

Irving and Delford Van Leuven sat on the porch of Charles and Maud Gardiner, located near the Traps in the town of Gardiner, in August 1911. The three men were bored and were trying to add some excitement to their day. Each idea they came up with just did not sound enticing enough to them. At one point, one of the men, most likely Delford Van Leuven, seized upon

Gunk Hideaway.
Today hikers get "lost"
in the vastness of the
Gunks. It was a place
where the wicked
could get lost, too.
Author's collection.

a horrifically wicked idea, which the men decided to enact—they would set the Shawangunk Mountains on fire. Delford Van Leuven perhaps came up with this plan because he had set a fire earlier, in May 1911.

All three men agreed that performing this destructive act would be stimulating to them as well as the community. The Van Leuvens set off for an area near the Mohonk Mountain House, and Gardiner voyaged in the other direction. Gardiner first stopped by a tool shed to gather a pair of "nippers." While the Van Leuvens were lighting the underbrush along Old Minnewaska Road with matches, it would be Gardiner's job to snip wires.

Even today, the Mohonk Mountain House has its own fire company, as fire has been no stranger to the area. In fact, in 1907, A.K. Smiley's illness was blamed on stress and nerves due to flames. A fire had been started by the berry pickers who, as mentioned, periodically ignited the forests in order to renew the crops that they depended upon for their livelihood. A fire set in 1907 had come perilously close to the mountain house.

Throughout the existence of the mountain house, fire has been a constant threat. In an effort to see forest fires and consequently extinguish them before they endangered the mountain house, a succession of fire towers was built. A fire tower is still visible from the village of New Paltz.

Skytop. This memorial fire tower was built for Alfred K. Smiley in the 1920s. *Courtesy of Library of Congress.*

Gardiner was charged with the mission of cutting the phone lines running from Mohonk so that the Smiley family, who owned the mountain resort, could not send out firefighters to put out the fire. It also prevented anyone in the community from calling up to Lake Mohonk. Once the fire got going, the three men gazed at it for a while. After they grew uninterested in watching the fire, it was reported in the newspapers that they soon all went to bed. What they did not know was that their excitement was to become a major nightmare, as the arsonists would be arrested and brought to jail in Kingston to face Judge Cantine.

An investigation was launched once it became apparent that the fire, which eventually was extinguished and spared Mohonk, was intentionally set. The New York State Conservation Commission sent detectives to scour the area for leads. One such detective was William H. Jackson, who worked for the New York State Fire Patrol. He was well acquainted with the Van Leuvens and the Traps where they lived. Jackson went undercover with

Mohonk Mountain House, founded by the Smiley Brothers in 1869. It is still in operation. *Courtesy of Library of Congress HABS/HAER.*

another officer and both boarded with the brother of Irving Van Leuven, Hiram. They posed as photographers for a moving-picture company. The two men worked to gain the trust of the Van Leuven men.

By October 1911, the detectives had enough evidence, according to a newspaper, to accuse the Van Leuvens and Gardiner with breaking forest, fish and game laws for igniting the forest fire along Old Minnewaska Road on August 13, 1911. Delford Van Leuven was also indicted for the fire he caused on May 16, 1911, in the same area. Ulster County Sheriff Deputies Cohen and Buddington arrested the men. The three arsonists were brought to the Ulster County Jail, where they were indicted before a grand jury on October 24, 1911. Their bail was set, with the highest amount being for Irving Van Leuven, who was also in trouble for breaking other fish and game laws.

When the trial opened in November 1911, an issue arose due to a lack of a confession; the men pled not guilty. However, a confession was finally obtained from Delford Van Leuven while he was in jail. The defense asked that the admission be thrown out because Delford Van Leuven claimed that it had been obtained under the threat of violence. This request was denied.

The trial continued as Charles and Maud Gardiner were brought in to testify. Another snafu occurred when there was speculation as to whether Charles Gardiner was offered twenty-five dollars by the prosecution to testify against the other two arsonists. Regardless, Delford Van Leuven was found guilty of starting the forest fires and was sentenced to one year in the Albany jail. Judge Cantine decided, however, that instead of putting him in jail, he would place him on probation for the duration of his sentence. Realizing that the cards were stacked against him, Irving Van Leuven decided to take the advice of his lawyer and change his plea to guilty. He was given a sentence of three months in the county jail.

CHAPTER 10

Arson in Kerhonkson

Today, the H.B. Humiston Funeral Home sits just off U.S. Route 209 on a street named, interestingly enough, Forty-second Street, like the world famous street in Times Square, New York City. It is situated in the tiny hamlet of Kerhonkson, located in the town of Wawarsing in Southwestern Ulster County. Over the more than one hundred years that it has been in existence, it has become somewhat of an institution in the hamlet; it is not just a funeral home but also somewhat of an historical landmark as well. One of the first female undertakers in New York State practiced her trade as a licensed undertaker here. Its founder, Howard Bryant Humiston, who died suddenly in 1940, would be proud of the business, as not only does his funeral home still stand in the historic hamlet of Kerhonkson, but the tradition of a husband and wife running the home also continues to this day.

The first owner of this business was Humiston. According to his obituary, Humiston was born in Napanoch, New York, which is located just south of Kerhonkson on U.S. Route 209. He was born in 1881 and started to pursue his interest in the business of undertaking after he moved to Kerhonkson with his wife, Margaret, whom he had married in 1904. Humiston was taken on as an apprentice with one of the most successful undertakers and furniture makers in Kerhonkson, a man by the name of Nathaniel W. Carman.

Carman was born in 1834. During those days, it was not uncommon for a furniture maker to make extra money by constructing coffins. This is probably the way Carman entered the undertaking business.

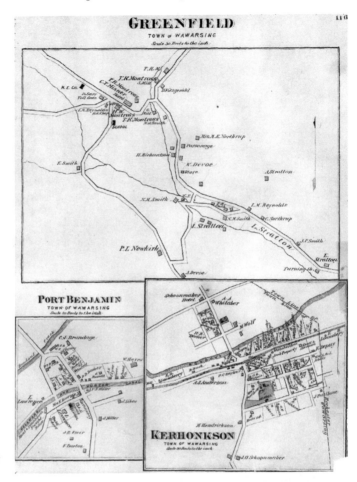

Map of Kerhonkson from the *Beers Atlas. Courtesy of Ulster County clerk's archive.*

Humiston started his apprenticeship with Carman in 1908. This most likely suited Carman because he was getting on in years, and as one of the most respected undertakers and most successful furniture makers in his area, he needed help when things became too busy. Humiston would spend the next year learning the funeral business from Carman.

Humiston learned his trade well, according to the *Kingston Daily Freeman*, as we shall see, perhaps all too well for Carman's liking. By the fall of 1908, Humiston felt confident enough to start his own funeral parlor business in Kerhonkson. He clearly felt that there was enough business for both himself and his teacher. The former had grown to like his adopted town.

Humiston was also part of a newer generation of undertakers that was starting to move away from just merely constructing coffins. During Carman's

Above: Old Iron Bridge. Recently replaced with a newer bridge, it was a landmark of Kerhonkson for many years. *Author's collection.*

Left: A later photo of H.B. Humiston, the owner of the funeral home located in Kerhonkson. The funeral home still bears his name and is located on Forty-second Street in downtown Kerhonkson. *Courtesy of Geoffrey and Heather Hazzard.*

day, the family went to a woodworker, who in turn took the measurements of the deceased. A coffin was then constructed, and roughly a day after the body was displayed for the family and close friends of the family to pay their respects, the body needed to be buried. With the advent of newer methods of embalming, the body could be kept longer by the family; this gave mourners enough time to have a service as well as a carriage ride to the cemetery. Prior to these newer embalming procedures, the body needed to be buried as quickly as possible.

Humiston not only provided more options to the bereaved, but he also offered what would become his trademark of compassionate services at a state-of-the-art funeral home. It became clear that he started to see himself as a funeral director and no longer an old-school undertaker or furniture maker. The people of Kerhonkson responded enthusiastically by giving the twenty-eight-year-old funeral director more of their business; this was much to the chagrin of Carman, who stood by wondering what he had created. Humiston could boast, as one newspaper printed, that from Kingston to Middletown, his funeral home was the most modern. The apprentice had become the competitor. What made matters even more difficult for Carman was that Humiston's business was located right across the street.

As Humiston continued to enhance his business by purchasing all of the needed expensive equipment, including a team of prize horses to pull a hearse, Carman became more and more jealous. Perhaps Carman felt betrayed by his apprentice, as Humiston's business was rapidly becoming so well known as one of the best in the area. When Humiston approached his old teacher and made an offer to buy out his business, Carmen's resentment toward Humiston festered into hatred. By all accounts, before this time, Carman was not a problematic individual in the community, and it was quite the contrary—he was well respected.

Carman decided that he needed to stop his former pupil from ruining him financially. On the evening of June 2, 1909, he waited until Humiston and his family went to bed. He watched, lingering, until the final light went out in the Humiston's house, indicating they were retiring for the evening. The last light was extinguished around 10:30 p.m., according to later accounts by Humiston. He and his wife had no reason to believe that in just about an hour, they would be roused from their slumber by their neighbor calling for them to come outside.

Mr. and Mrs. Jason Decker were also in bed about the same time as their neighbors, the Humistons. Mrs. Decker was the first to hear the start of the night's activities. She heard the horses whinnying from the barn. Mrs. Decker remained in bed listening, hoping that perhaps the horses would settle down. Their whinnying did not subside but rather grew louder. Someone or something was bothering the horses, and their cries grew louder and more frantic. She woke up her husband, as now she believed that someone was trying to steal their horses. The husband and wife dressed as quickly as they could; Decker then ran out of their house, which was just a few hundred feet from the Humistons' barn. He found the old Lounsberry Barn, where Humiston kept his equipment and prize horses, fully engulfed by fire. The old Lounsberry Barn was at that time owned by James Lundrigan.

A crowd was quickly forming as Mr. and Mrs. Humiston were roused from bed. Humiston stood in disbelief as he watched the barn burn. The flames coming from the barn were so intense on that June morning that embers were floating in the air and created the possibility of a larger fire igniting. If allowed to grow unchecked, this fire could consume the entire village. Individuals scrambled to extinguish the flames, forming what a newspaper referred to as a bucket brigade. Decker grabbed a ladder in an effort to put out embers endangering the parsonage as well as the church. He directed that the house and barn of another neighbor, which was about two hundred yards from the Humistons' barn, also had to be protected. Decker was able to secure a hand pump to assist in cooling the roofs of the houses that were beginning to burn.

Decker and others struggled to extinguish the barn fire, as did Humiston, who could not be held back. He rushed into the flames in an attempt to save his prize horses or any equipment. He found himself repelled again and again by the intensity of the heat and smoke of the fire. Finally, he found a way into the barn.

Once in the barn, Humiston saw a burlap bag, which he investigated because it seemed to be so out of place and he did not recognize it. Upon closer examination, he discovered that it had been saturated with oil and powder that had not yet ignited. Shortly after finding the burlap bag, it exploded and injured Humiston quite severely. However, he was undeterred.

Humiston made his way to a barrel of water that he kept filled in the barn. Once he made it to the barrel, he found that it too had been contaminated with oil. Humiston tried the hand pump nearby only to realize that it had been disconnected—this was the obvious work of an arsonist! But who and why?

The barn was a total loss. Humiston's prize horses were dead, a large amount of equipment was ruined and Humiston himself was burned from the explosion. Howard B. Humiston offered $500 as a reward for the capture of the arsonist. Talk circulated throughout the town about the barrel containing oil, the burlap bag with oil and powder and the disconnected water pump. Almost immediately, Carman came under suspicion.

Everything in Humiston's barn was insured, except for his prize horses. He had an insurance policy of $1,500 taken out with the Continental Insurance Company, but the insurance company reported that his losses were upward of $2,500. He used the insurance money he received to rebuild his business. He was determined to send a message to the arsonist that this was not going to deter him from running his company. The Humiston Funeral Home eventually began to recover and slowly started to recoup its losses. It was clear that the intention of the arsonist was to send a message to Humiston— he wanted him to get out of the funeral business.

All was quiet for the next three years, from 1909 to 1912. However, little did Humiston know that in the mind of Carman, the issue was far from finished. Humiston had his suspicions, as did some of his neighbors. One neighbor in particular, Mrs. Gillespie, kept her eye on Carman. This did not deter Carman, who decided in his warped mind that things had settled down enough to finish what he had started three years earlier. What he did not count on was the watchful eye of Mrs. Gillespie.

The evening of January 30, 1912, Humiston decided to go to a meeting of the American Mechanics a short distance from his home. Seventy-eight-year-old Carman waited patiently for night to fall. He watched as Humiston left his home with Mr. Gillespie. There is no indication that anyone else was home at the Humiston house. While Mr. Humiston was away, Mrs. Gillespie kept an eye on his property when she saw the aged undertaker walking with two containers that she could see were filled with oil. She felt that this was not a good turn of events, especially since she might have known that a large quantity of oil was found in the burning barn three years earlier. It was also out of the ordinary that Carman would need this amount of oil, especially at this hour of the night.

Mrs. Gillespie hurried out of her home to where her husband and Humiston were attending a dinner. Once she found both gentlemen, she explained what she had just witnessed and said she was sure that Carman was up to no good. The two men left immediately and headed toward Humiston's property. When the two arrived, Humiston was in disbelief at what he was witnessing. He watched as Carman took pieces of paper, methodically saturated them with oil and then carefully placed them on the floor. This time, he would make no mistakes like he did in the barn. He poured all of the remaining oil in the containers all over the floor; these were the same containers Mrs. Gillespie had described to her husband and Humiston.

Humiston had seen all that he could stand. He did not want to give Carman the opportunity to light a match and start the fire. He had witnessed enough to put this man away for life. He entered the same room as Carman, who now knew he had been caught in the act. Humiston confronted his old teacher but was unprepared for what came next.

Carman would not allow himself to be caught, as he believed that it was only Humiston and himself in the room or outside. The old man drew a pistol threatening to kill Humiston if he tried to stop him. John Gary, a neighbor, heard the commotion and saw that Carman had a gun pointed at Humiston. He entered the area and wrestled Carman to the ground, gaining possession of the pistol. Once the gun was secured, Gary thought it best if he escorted Carman home; he gave Carman instructions to stay there until the morning when someone would come and get him. Newspaper accounts do not mention the whereabouts of Gillespie during this time.

The following morning, Carman was brought before Wawarsing Justice James Van Etten. The justice directed that the seventy-eight-year-old furniture maker/businessman be placed in jail. The case ultimately ended up before Ulster County Judge Charles F. Cantine, who denied a request by Carman's lawyer for bail so that his client could return home while awaiting trial. He deemed the old man a danger to the community. It was reported in a newspaper at the time that it was believed that Carman could easily make bail because he was worth about $100,000. The judge refused and ordered that Carman be evaluated by two doctors named A. Vrooman and E.M. Loughram. They ultimately found, in their opinions, that Carman was insane because of hardening of the arteries; thus, they felt that he was incompetent and unable to stand trial.

As a result, Carman's case did not go to trial. It was recommended that he be sent to the state insane asylum in Middletown, located in Orange County, New York. Humiston was incensed that Carman was not sentenced to the facility for the criminally insane in Mattawan, New Jersey. Judge Cantine explained to Humiston that because he was not indicted in a court of law, he could not be treated as criminally insane.

Carman ultimately was committed to the state asylum in Middletown. A newspaper reported on February 5, 1912, that Carman was "very sad" that he had committed this act against his former student. The paper continued that he realized now that it was not the way to resolve his personal grudge.

Carman would never be released from his confinement from the state asylum. He died in December 1912; where he was buried is not stated in the newspapers of the day. A lawsuit ensued against Carman's estate to recover the insurance money that had been paid out to Humiston in 1909. Humiston continued to prosper in his town of Kerhonkson, eventually becoming a well-respected coroner in Ulster County. He held that position until his death in 1940. He eventually relocated his Kerhonkson business to the site it occupies today, across from the Federated Church on Forty-second Street in downtown Kerhonkson. It still functions as a successful funeral home and still bears his name.

The Day Kingston was Put to the Torch

In the fall of 1777, the British were stunned that one of the strongest armies and navies in the world had still not crushed the rebellion in its North America colonies. The war was now in its second year in the American colonies. A British general named John Burgoyne believed that he had the final solution to end the rebellion once and for all—he proposed cutting off the New England colonies, such as New York, from the rest of the colonies. Burgoyne felt that the New England colonies, specifically Massachusetts, were at the heart of the rebellion against the crown. He reasoned that isolating Massachusetts would be tantamount to severing the head of a snake and rendering the rest of its body useless. Furthermore, if Burgoyne could segregate the New England colonies by gaining control of the Hudson River, the flow of both communications and supplies to these areas could be stopped.

Burgoyne proposed accomplishing this plan with the assistance of three armies; he would lead one, and Colonel Barry St. Ledger and General Howe would lead the others. St. Ledger and Burgoyne would march from Canada. It was hoped that the third prong of the attack, headed by Howe, would sail from New York City in order to reinforce the other approaching armies.

Howe ultimately ended up marching on Philadelphia and defeated the rebels at Brandywine and Germantown. He left another general, General Clinton, in charge of a small force to assist his army if need be. This left the two armies coming out of Canada to take control of the Hudson at Albany. St. Ledger was stopped at Fort Stanwix, and Burgoyne, after taking over Fort Ticonderoga, saw his fortune take a turn, especially after the Battle

Hudson Highlands. Colonel Jonathan Hasbrouck lived just outside the exit to the Hudson Highlands. It is known for its ruggedness. The British would have come through this passage. *Author's collection.*

Hasbrouck House. The home of Colonel Jonathan Hasbrouck and his wife, Tryntje DuBois. Today, it is a historic site in Newburgh. *Courtesy of Library of Congress.*

of Bennington. Once his Native American allies left and he lost a large number of soldiers in Bennington, it became apparent that Burgoyne was in trouble. General Vaughn in New York City was dispatched up the Hudson to hopefully assist Burgoyne or at the least act as a diversion.

Above: The Hudson River was a superhighway for communication and supplies, and the British did their best to gain control of it. Their hopes were dashed by 1777. *Courtesy of Library of Congress.*

Right: Jane McCrea was killed on her way to visit her fiancé in the British lines. She was killed by Native American allies. Her death became a rallying point for militia. *Courtesy of Library of Congress.*

Meanwhile, in a stone house overlooking the Hudson River just outside the Hudson Highlands, was the home of Colonel Jonathan Hasbrouck. A militia colonel, he was instrumental in the construction of the twin river forts known as Forts Montgomery and Clinton. These two forts had been

A Tory's day of judgment. Tories were not treated well when caught, especially after the burning of Kingston. *Courtesy of Library of Congress.*

erected through 1776 in order to fortify the Hudson River. The first chain of defense was strong across the Hudson; this included *cheveaux de frise*, which were boxes, constructed with wood and filled with rocks, that had spikes jutting out from their centers at an angle. They were sunk in the river in an effort to puncture hulls of boats that made it past the chain.

The forts were attacked by Vaughn on October 6, 1777. Eventually, letters and individuals arrived alerting Hasbrouck to what was going on. He was, at the very least, aware that prior to this, the Hudson Valley was preparing for an inevitable attack. A letter from another Clinton, Governor Clinton, rebuked Hasbrouck for not meeting his quota of troops to defend the Hudson River from the British. However, as pointed out by Hasbrouck in a letter to Governor Clinton, he was convalescing after a serious illness almost killed him. He was in no condition to respond to the alarms to lead an army in defense of Kingston or Newburgh.

The attack flotilla was nearing Newburgh, according to the *Public Papers of George Clinton*, on October 15, 1777. There was a real fear that the British might come ashore to sack the important military depot of Newburgh and/or raid the important mills in the area. Additionally, Newburgh was the home of Hasbrouck and his family, and there was concern that the British might attack the home of such a noted patriot.

According to family legend, and written about in Ralph Lefevre's *History of New Paltz,* in response to this turn of events, Hasbrouck reached out to his eighteen-year-old daughter, Rachel. When she arrived, he explained the grim situation to her and asked that she gather all the valuables that she could carry and bring them inland to the home where her father grew up outside of New Paltz, in an area known as Guilford. At the time, the home belonged to Hasbrouck's oldest brother, Abraham.

Rachel did as she was told by her father and collected their family's treasures. Once this was done, she went out to the barn to saddle her horse, named Firefly. She took the road from Newburgh to her father's boyhood home in Guilford. It is related in the story that this road was a rough one, marked by "slashes in the trees."

Room of Seven Doors and One Window, one of the most famous rooms in American history. It might have been here that Colonel Jonathan Hasbrouck spoke. The British ships could have been seen from the window looking out at today's Mount Beacon. *Author's collection.*

Mount Beacon and Hudson River. This mountain once had signal fires on top of it. It is largely the way Jonathan Hasbrouck would have seen it. *Courtesy of Library of Congress.*

Rachel did not get very far for along her way before a band of Tories, hoping to aid the British invasion of the Hudson Valley, stopped her. Lefevre wrote that the leader of the Tories believed that Rachel was very pretty and that no one should harm her. He continued that as the party of Tories tried to figure out what to do with Rachel, she decided to make a run for it. Rachel smacked her horse and took off in a hail of pistol fire. She presumably made the rest of the trip inland without incident.

Newburgh was never ransacked, and contrary to family legend, the Hasbrouck house was not fired upon as the family huddled in the basement, as it is said that the cannonballs fell short. James Donnelly, whose recollections were published in E.M. Ruttenber's *History of Newburgh*, recalled when the British came up the Hudson River. He was a small boy living in Newburgh in 1777. Donnelly recalled that during that time, people in the community hid their valuables in the woods. When it became obvious that the British had broken through the defensive chain, he also remembered his mother taking him into the cellar of their house. While down there, he recalled hearing cannons being fired and the balls falling short. Perhaps at a later time, someone attributed this anecdote to the Hasbrouck family. There is no indication that cannons were fired at the Hasbrouck house or that Hasbrouck's home was singled out for any kind of retribution.

As alarms continued to sound, British ships made their way past Newburgh on their way toward Kingston, New York. Kingston, located in the Mid-

Inside Hasbrouck House. The staircase leading to two rooms upstairs is located in the newer part of the home, built in 1770. *Courtesy of Library of Congress HABS/HAER.*

Hudson Valley's Ulster County, has been known for many things during its long history. It was once a center of commerce, where valuable goods were shipped up and down the Hudson River. It was also renowned for producing magnificent wheat. Conversely, the British regarded Kingston as "a nursery for almost every villain in the country," which helped to justify their invasions.

In 1777, New York created its first constitution, thus forming the state of New York. The new government of this state met in Kingston because it had been forced north when the British invaded New York City. In Kingston, this new constitution created a senate, governor, assembly and judiciary. Kingston was also declared New York State's first capital in 1777. In fact, New York State's first senate met at what is today Clinton

Senate House. *Courtesy of Library of Congress HABS/HAER.*

Street in Kingston. Initially, the senate met in the home of Abraham Van Gaasbeek from September to October 1777. The New York State Assembly, meanwhile, met at the Bogardus Tavern, while the judiciary met at the courthouse.

The New York State Senate, as well as the residents of Kingston, was forced to flee in October 1777 in advance of Vaughn's expedition; they had been evacuating since early October. Burgoyne was ultimately defeated, and on October 16, 1777, the British, under the command of Vaughn, put Kingston to the torch. One of the buildings burned by the British was that where the senate had met. Luckily, the records of the new government had earlier been sent farther inland, to what is today Kerhonkson, to be stored at the home of Johannes Hardenberg. His home stood near the corner of U.S. 209 and State Highway 44/55. The remains of the city of Kingston were also torched by the British.

One of those individuals directly affected by this British invasion was Abraham, the brother of Jonathan Hasbrouck. Abraham Hasbrouck was one of the richest men in Ulster Country and was a colonel in the Ulster County militia, like his brother. Throughout most of his life, Abraham Hasbrouck kept a diary. In his accounts, he kept records of deaths, noteworthy weather events and significant personal events, such as the burning of Kingston, the place where he had resided since the 1730s. This diary is a valuable resource

Hardenberg House. Long since demolished, it was considered a unique home but not preserved in time. Parts of the home were taken for display in a museum. *Courtesy of Library of Congress HABS/HAER.*

Elemendorf House. It was opposite this tavern, it is believed, that the Bogardus Tavern stood for many years. It was also where the New York State Assembly met in 1777. *Courtesy of Library of Congress.*

to use when researching how the war and torching of Kingston took quite a toll on one of the area's most prominent citizens.

Abraham Hasbrouck recorded that in 1776, he lost his home to fire in British-occupied New York City. During the same year, his home in Kingston also burned, though this was deemed an accident by Abraham Hasbrouck. In May 1777, Abraham Hasbrouck moved into a new dwelling in Kingston; in October of the same year, this home was set on fire by the British. His own sons tried to oppose the landing of the British troops, but their efforts were futile.

According to Abraham Hasbrouck's diary, he not only lost his house but also two barns, a cider house, a library, furniture and a small outdoor kitchen. All that was spared in his town, according to his writings, were one home and a barn. The British also seized three of Abraham Hasbrouck's slaves, named Harry, Janey and Flora. All told, he recorded his monetary losses at around £10,000.

Once Kingston was destroyed, the invading Vaughn continued north up the Hudson River and stopped to burn the home of the Livingstons. The Livingston family had enough advance notice that they were able to escape after hiding all of their valuables. Vaughn ordered that the Livingston mansion, named Clermont, be torched to the ground.

The surrender at Saratoga is considered to be the turning point in the American Revolution. After Saratoga, the French became allies of the United States. *Courtesy of Library of Congress.*

Saratoga American defenses. *Courtesy of Library of Congress.*

Tarred and feathered. *Courtesy of Library of Congress.*

Dreams of ending the war with a decisive blow and controlling the Hudson soon ended for the British. Burgoyne was defeated at Saratoga and there was the existence of a French alliance with the United States of America. After burning the Livingstons' mansion on October 19, 1777, Vaughn retreated back to New York City, which the British would retain until the end of the war.

After the Battle of Saratoga, the wickedness of the British foray up the Hudson was fresh in everyone's minds, as was the burning of the beloved town of Kingston. Hessian prisoners of war were on their way to Newburgh, where they would lodge with the Hasbrouck family. These Hessian mercenaries embodied the wickedness of the British government who employed these foreigners to put down the rebellion in North America. Once these Hessian prisoners of war left Newburgh, the wicked invasion of Vaughn and the torching of Kingston soon drifted into memory as the war continued on.

CHAPTER 12

Il Mano Nero

The Black Hand

A s New York City continued to grow in the late nineteenth century into the early twentieth century, so did the demand for water for its citizens. They needed not only water but also a clean source of water. Pushing this growth was wave after wave of immigrants coming mainly from Southern and Eastern Europe. New York City decided that the cheapest and most logical place to obtain the clean water it so desired was the Catskill Mountains in Upstate New York. It was decided that six reservoirs would be built in this area. The first of these to be built was the Ashokan in Ulster County. The Ashokan became the largest manmade lake in Ulster County. According to an article in the *New York Times*, "Aboriginal Ulster," the project was only equaled by the Panama Canal.

A *Hudson Valley Magazine* article from 2008 placed the whole endeavor in perspective: "1,000 acres of farm land vanished…Eleven villages were forcibly evacuated and burned to the ground to make room for the 83,000-acres body of water—at the time, the world's largest reservoir." The ash from the burnt houses needed to be carted away. Even stumps of trees needed to be removed and burned out of the ground. Additionally, countless cemeteries had to be located, and the interred had to be unearthed and relocated. Even today, when you gaze over the Ashokan, considering the time period, it was an engineering feat that boggles the mind.

Massive amounts of both skilled and unskilled laborers were needed to help with this monumental feat. In New York City, there were millions of immigrants looking for not only steady work but also a way out of the

Working on the Ashokan, a mammoth operation compared to the building of the Panama Canal. It caused the forced removal of many people, as well as the towns they lived in, at the time New York City purchased their properties. *Author's collection.*

awful slums some of them inhabited in the city. A considerable number of immigrants made their way from New York City to the Catskills to work on the Ashokan, setting up towns in the process. Just as when they arrived in New York City, their cultures were in some ways shocking to the residents living around the reservoir.

A.J. Loftin writes, "A workers' camp rapidly arose on the southern slope of Winchell Hill near the town of Brown's Station. The camp had running water, electricity, paved streets, a sewage disposal plant, a hospital, and garbage collection. It became customary for locals to drive to the camp on Sundays to inspect their odd new neighbors."

Ulster County citizens looked on in horror as all of the problems associated with work camps started to rear their ugly heads, such as drinking establishments, houses of prostitution, gambling and, in some cases, violent crime. One newspaper reported that shootings were quite commonplace, as was rampant cocaine use. Crime in general usually picked up in the warmer months and kept police busy in places such as High Falls.

In some cases, these work camps were like small cities. They peaked in population in the summer, when the population in some camps could be as high as seven thousand. When work slowed in the winter, the number of workers could drop to less than half that. When the men were done

Members of the Black Hand. *Courtesy of Library of Congress.*

with their shifts working on the dam, there was, in many cases, nothing else to do but drink or gamble. It was reported in the *New York Times* that the consumption of alcohol by laborers was forbidden, as well as its sale in the labor camps; however, this was probably unenforceable, or perhaps some of the heads of the camps looked the other way.

These same individuals claimed that, in their opinion, a considerable amount of the alcohol being sold was from the residents of the surrounding towns looking to make some extra money. Yet another article purported that there were some fifty drinking establishments within a fifteen-mile stretch of road. Once again, besides alcohol, weapons and violence were other problems. Local police forces such as the one in High Falls had their hands full with workers coming into town against the rules of the Board of Water Supply Police, the police force that was given the role by New York City to patrol the area around the future reservoir.

A tremendous fear attached to the influx of Italian immigrants was the Black Hand Society, which was already creating what was bordering on hysteria in New York City and as far away as Buffalo. During the time that the Ashokan was being constructed, newspapers ran daily articles on the work of the Black Hand. One of these papers, the *Kingston Daily Freeman,* wrote that this society originated in New York City. It was of Sicilian origin and was an organization built on crime, especially toward other Italian immigrants. The group used murder and intimidation to exact money from its victims and sometimes also took revenge on those who insulted the honor of the organization. Their dreaded instrument was the Black Hand Letter, which sometimes had a black hand drawn at the bottom of the letter, a reference to the society, or was written in blood-red ink.

The article believed that society was also called the Family. The Family, like the Mafia, had a leadership that was broken down into three tiers. The wise master was at the highest level, and the lowest ranking member was the Ysung of Honor. It was believed that in 1909, the leader of the Black Hand in Manhattan was Angelo Chario of 123 Mulberry Street in New York City, which was part of an area known as Little Italy.

According to an article written for the *North American Review* in 1908 by Gaetano D'Amato entitled "The Black Hand Myth," D'Amato believed that the Black Hand was a myth that was created in the United States. He also believed it was not an organized entity like, say, the late Mafia. The *idea* of the Black Hand was used more for extortion rather than it being an actual criminal organization. The term itself was used to invoke terror.

Demetrio Zema, age twenty-seven, was one of the immigrants who journeyed to Ulster County to work in the camps. According to Zema, he was originally from Katonah in Westchester County in New York. He ran a business there and made a living but was by no means doing well. He claimed that in 1908, he was sent a note called a Black Hand Letter; it stated that if he wanted to live, he would need to put $100 in an envelope and send it to the address indicated in the letter. Zema knew that this letter was indeed from a member of the Black Hand because of the fact that not only was there a black hand at the end of the letter but also it was written in red ink…or blood. Fearing for his life, he decided it would be best if he moved.

When Zema heard that there was work on the Ashokan, he moved to an area known as Brown's Station, where he was employed by Superintendent John S. Lowry. Zema was later fired by the subcontractor Lowry, which created problems between the two men. Zema, needing to make a living, decided to rent a saloon from a local individual by the name of Ike Carman. It was Zema's hope that he could sell beer and other alcohol to the laborers working on the Ashokan. However, the saloon, which occupied a bluff overlooking Lowry's house on the road to Marbletown, ended up becoming a source of annoyance for him.

Zema was originally from Elizabeth, New Jersey, and in fact, had been born there; he claimed that he changed his name to Demetrio Zema from Luigi Fogia because he wanted to throw the people hunting him off of his trail. He stated again and again that he feared for his life because of what had happened in Katonah. By all accounts, he ran a somewhat successful boardinghouse and saloon with his wife.

One day in February 1909, an individual by the name of Gaetano Arrigo arrived at Brown's Station looking for work on the new reservoir being built. This area was under the jurisdiction of Lowry. Arrigo did not speak much English and was not a skilled laborer, but he listed himself as a shovel and cable worker. Lowry did not hire Arrigo, so he again went looking for work. During his time looking for employment, Arrigo decided to board at Zema's. If he was not working for Lowry, he could not stay in the camp. He thus stayed at Zema's before actually being hired by him to help with work around the boardinghouse.

Sometime around the time that Arrigo appeared looking for work, Zema started having trouble making money; by his accounts, he was only making about fifty cents a day. This was because Lowry decided to order laborers in the Brown's Station camp not to drink at the boardinghouse owned by Zema and told them that if they were caught, their employment would be immediately terminated. Thus, Zema's customers dropped off quickly. Why Lowry decreed this is open to conjecture. Some felt that he did not like Arrigo or Zema. Still others believed that Lowry was a "temperance man." This was a slang term for someone who subscribed to the Temperance Movement, most notably those who maintained that alcohol should not be consumed. It was this group that was influential in the passage of the Eighteenth Amendment to the United States Constitution, which outlawed alcohol consumption and sale until 1933.

The events of April 26, 1909, are debated by all involved, but one thing is for sure: someone tried to burn down the home of Lowry in the early morning hours of the twenty-sixth. This was done while people were in the home sleeping, thus making the act an attempted murder as well as arson. In addition to Lowry and his family, two other individuals were present in the house that night: Clayvest Cross and Fred W. Minson. The two men were roused out of their beds by the smell of smoke and ran outside to encounter fire on the side of the house. The two men quickly found buckets and were credited with saving the structure by putting out the flames before they had a chance to really take off.

There was no doubt that someone had intentionally set this fire. A watchman was placed at the home for the safety of all involved. An investigation was then launched to ascertain who was responsible for this almost tragic event. Meanwhile, the plot only thickened as individuals pointed fingers at each other. There was also fear among people in the area around the Ashokan that the Black Hand was somehow involved in the attack on Lowry.

Two private detectives were hired by Lowry to investigate the assault on his home. One was named Albert Captillano, who was twenty-three years old and was from Albany. Captillano was a cigar maker by trade but decided that he wanted to become a private detective; for the past two years, he had been employed by the Humphrey's Central Detective Agency in Albany. He went undercover in the Brown's Station camp to see what kind of information he could unearth on the torching of the Lowry home. When not working at the camp, Captillano boarded at Zema's. While there, he discovered that there was ample evidence of some kind of altercation existing between Zema and Lowry.

The other detective working the case, Joe DeVivo, was also from Albany and also worked for Humphrey's Central Detective Agency. He, too, tried to gain the trust of Zema in order to see what he could find out about the whole Lowry arson attempt. On June 24, this detective also decided to pay the Zema boardinghouse a visit.

What the two detectives found was a disgruntled saloonkeeper; possibly because the two men were Italian, Zema felt he could confide in them. DeVivo spoke Italian and might have convinced Zema to talk with him. He also posed as a criminal on the lam from nearby Rochester where he claimed he had killed a man who disagreed with him on how to divide money that they had stolen. DeVivo even went so far as to flash signs that he believed only a person who belonged to the Black Hand Society would know and use. He was surprised when the saloonkeeper flashed these signs back at him.

Zema, in company of the detective, admitted to wanting to kill Lowry for no other reason than that he felt that the man was destroying his business. He knew that Lowry was afraid of him, and he told the detective that one day he would murder the man, and Lowry knew it. He explained that he had offered the subcontractor money if he allowed him to serve the men who worked in his camp. The superintendent did not budge, so Zema felt that since he was in the way, he just needed to be removed from the equation. Perhaps the next superintendent would be a little bit more sympathetic to his cause. Zema also admitted that he was the one who had set fire to Lowry's house. While the two men spoke, they learned that Zema had an assistant of sorts, albeit a reluctant one.

Later, during Zema's testimony in front of Judge Cantine, he admitted that he had voiced to Arrigo, one of his boarders and workers, that Lowry was a problem. Arrigo testified that Zema asked him to assist with arrangements necessary to get rid of Lowry. Arrigo obliged because he was very fearful of Zema and what he was capable of.

The detectives were on the scene only to find out about the Lowry fire affair, but the other stories they heard made them think that they had a really dangerous man on their hands in Brown's Station. Zema told a story about shooting a man in Katonah. When DeVivo checked out the story, he found out that not only was the story true, but that there was still a warrant out for Zema's arrest. The man he sat with was wanted for being an attempted murderer and had served time for assault as well. There were other stories circulating that Zema hoped would make the impression that he was a very bad individual; Lowry picked the wrong man to play with this time.

The detectives notified the authorities in Ulster County about the arson attempt on Lowry's home and meanwhile took Zema to Westchester to answer the charges on his old warrant. On July 4, when Deputy Sheriff William Cohen arrived to arrest both Zema and Arrigo, the former had been back in Ulster County. Cohen was accompanied by aqueduct policemen.

When the men arrived at Zema's saloon, Cohen knocked on the door and was told by Zema that they were closed. When he knocked even more forcefully, the man opened the door. Cohen read the arrest warrant to Zema and as he moved to apprehend him, Zema jumped back and reached for his pistol to shoot Cohen. One of the other detectives helped subdue Zema; at this point, his wife attempted to grab a pistol but was also restrained by law enforcement. Cohen also arrested Zema's alleged accomplice Arrigo and placed him in the Ulster County Jail to wait trial.

Zema ultimately ended up in the Westchester County Jail because the warrant against him for attempted murder was older than the one sworn out against him in Kingston, Ulster County. Cohen and a private detective from Kingston went to retrieve the man for an October trial. It was reported by the detective that when Cohen left his seat for a moment and was out of earshot, Zema made threats against the individuals who were accusing him of torching Lowry's home. Zema said the same things to Cohen when the detective wasn't in their company.

The trial of Demetrio Zema opened up on a Wednesday morning in October 1909 in front of Judge Cantine in Kingston. Unbeknownst to Zema, Arrigo had agreed to a plea deal to testify against his old boss. Zema was represented by attorney John J. Hughes from the law firm of Hughes and

Holden located in White Plains, Westchester County. Attorney Hughes knew Zema because he had previously represented him in his assault case. The prosecution was represented by Ulster County District Attorney Cunningham. It was the contention of the district attorney for Ulster County that it was indeed Zema who had acted to burn down the home of Lowry; Arrigo helped his boss because he was afraid that he was capable of murder.

The public was captivated as the tales of the Black Hand circulated. Zema's attorney asked the judge for a bail hearing, which Judge Cantine refused, citing that Zema, in his opinion, was probably one of the most dangerous men in Ulster County. Extra security had to be added to the courtroom during the trial out of fear that the many men believed to be of Italian descent could be capable of violence or were members of the Black Hand. Mrs. Zema was searched daily by the jailer's wife because of threats she had made in the courtroom against the star witness, her husband's employee. His wife, at one point during the trial, yelled that if she had a pistol, it would be her pleasure to kill him on the spot, saying that she would gladly shoot him dead and be happy to do twenty years in prison as a result. Eventually, Mrs. Zema was barred from the courtroom altogether because of her outbursts during the trial.

The cards were stacked against Zema from the outset, as witness after witness corroborated the stories that it was Zema who wished to burn down the house of Lowry and that he wished him dead. Zema had told too many people about his ambition to kill the man. Lowry testified that he had some problems with Zema in the past and that Zema had offered to bribe him for the right to sell alcohol to the laborers working under Lowry. He refused, which he believed set off the chain of events with Zema. There was a fear at one point that Lowry and Attorney Hughes were destined to have issues, as Hughes accused Lowry of not telling the entire truth and insinuated that he might be prejudiced toward his client. There was a heated discussion in the hotel across the street between the two men. At one point, Lowry asked Hughes to remove his glasses so that they could settle this outside. Hughes backed down and profusely apologized for his accusations.

Perhaps the most damaging witness against Zema was Arrigo. Everything that Arrigo said checked out and corroborated with other witnesses. He claimed that Zema was angry at Lowry because Zema had offered him twenty-five cents for every barrel of alcohol he sold if Lowry would just allow him to sell alcohol to the laborers who worked under him. Lowry turned the offer down flat, and Zema was enraged because without the men drinking, he would be ruined.

A dynamite shed like this is probably where Zema stored the dynamite he never was able to use. *Courtesy of Library of Congress.*

According to Arrigo, Zema asked him to steal some dynamite from the worksite of Lowry and bring it to the boardinghouse. It was not used that night, but placed in Zema's cellar. At one point, District Attorney Cunningham requested that the dynamite from Zema's cellar be brought into the courtroom as evidence, but that request was overruled by Judge Cantine. After the dynamite was examined by explosive experts, it was found to be leaking and unstable, so they feared that it could detonate and kill everyone in the courtroom.

Arrigo continued to testify that on the night of the twenty-sixth, he saw Zema with a tomato can full of kerosene and a shotgun, as well as a small box. Zema told Arrigo to come with him, and the two men walked over to Lowry's house. Zema handed him a breech-loading double-barreled shotgun, which he identified. According to testimony, Zema left Arrigo about thirty paces from the house with the gun and gave him the order that if anybody came walking down the road, he was to blast them. Zema went toward the house and doused it with the kerosene he had in the can, and soon after, there were flames. He told Arrigo if they could not burn the house down that night, they would simply have to come back to finish the job, probably using dynamite. When asked why he went along with the sick plot, Arrigo exclaimed that he was scared of Zema and feared for his life.

Attorney Hughes questioned the witness, who spoke to Cunningham in his office through an interpreter on July 8 or 9. He told the same story to the district attorney that he had told on the stand. Hughes did not have a problem with this, but what he did take issue with was that Arrigo had told his brother-in-law Opedisimo Casemo that he had lied in order to avoid prosecution, and if he found that he could not be prosecuted, he would recant his version of that night's events. Hughes also wondered if Arrigo might have been motivated out of love for the defendant's wife. He claimed that Arrigo had made it known to Mrs. Zema that her husband would go away for twenty-five years, and it would thus make sense for her to take up with him. If she refused his offer, he would make sure that he "fixed" Zema for good. Arrigo denied that this conversation ever took place.

Both detectives were also brought to the stand to discuss what they had learned about Zema and his alleged torching of the house. Special attention was spent on Detective DeVivo—the defense attorney asked if he had any kind of special relationship with the Zemas, which he denied. The attorney asked about a letter that was purportedly sent to Mrs. Zema from Zema about how to testify. He denied that any such letter existed and affirmed that he was not paid any money by the Zemas. He also denied that he brought any money to Zema while he was in jail as a favor to his wife.

The high point in the trial occurred when Zema finally took the stand. The newspapers during that time reported that he spoke English well. He talked fast and always looked at the people in the crowd and the jury. He claimed to not have known why he was on trial until the train ride back when he questioned the two men charged with bringing him to Kingston for trial. Zema believed it was Arrigo who set the house on fire because he told Zema that he was angry that Lowry would not talk to him. Zema begged his boarder to drop the situation because he felt that if Lowry found out, it could become trouble for him and his business. Zema went on to say that Arrigo could not just let things go and felt disrespected by Lowry.

Zema continued to say that he never approached Lowry, but rather that Lowry came into his saloon to ask who rented him his place. When Zema replied to the question, Lowry told him that he better move from the area because he would not do well there at all. In an effort to try and win over Lowry, Zema went across the way to his house with three fine bottles of whiskey, which Lowry refused because he was a temperance man. Zema even asked Lowry if he wanted to be his partner in the saloon and boardinghouse, but again Lowry refused; however, he did say that if Zema wanted to stay in business, he would have to pay him money each month. This is a charge that John S. Lowry flatly refused under oath when he took the stand.

Zema was ultimately found guilty by the jury of first-degree arson. On the day of his sentencing, Zema's attorney made a plea for leniency for his client. He asked that he be sent to a reformatory and not to a prison. He continued to say that this would be sufficient punishment, as Zema's life had all but been destroyed and he would find it hard to make a living now. He also pointed out that he had been in jail for several months and this should be taken into consideration with his sentencing. The judge ended up sentencing Zema to twelve to fifteen years at Dannemora Prison with hard labor. When he boarded a train for the long trip to Dannemora, Zema reportedly said to Sheriff Boice, "Goodbye, Sheriff. I'll come back here when I get out." No one mentioned if they thought that this could be a threat.

Zema's wife, it was thought, faced deportation back to Italy because of the part she played in the whole affair, including her threats to get even with those who put her husband in jail. She had told her husband when he was in jail that she wished to return to Croton in Westchester County. The papers wrote that although the Zemas claimed to be married, it was doubtful that they were actually husband and wife, and this could also be a reason for deportation. There would be little worry from her husband because he was far enough away to not cause problems.

After the trial, it was rumored that Zema's boardinghouse also doubled as a house of prostitution. There was an appeal of Zema's conviction, which was handled by DeWitt W. Ostrander of Clintondale, in Ulster County. The appeal was put forth by some friends who felt that Zema was treated too harshly by the court. Ultimately, the conviction of the lower court was upheld, and Zema remained in Dannemora to finish out his sentence.

CHAPTER 13

Gyp the Blood and the Ulster County Connection

During the turn of the century, New York City could be a tough place. The area around present-day Times Square, known as the Tenderloin, was particularly dangerous. This place was ripe with gambling, prostitution and establishments that served alcohol.

The city did its best to get the matters under control with the use of the New York City Police Department. Police Commissioner Waldo even went so far as to create a special vice squad with Lieutenant Charles Becker at its head. He was charged with the mission to not only crack down on the illegal activities mentioned above but to also seek out the individuals who profited from them by way of extortion, pickpocketing or graft. What Waldo did not count on was that the man in charge of this operation quickly became part of the problem.

Becker was taking kickbacks to ensure protection from raids by his squad of enforcers. He also became partial owner of some illegitimate establishments in exchange for protection. When he would later be brought to justice for all of his wrongdoings, the veteran New York City police officer would become the only officer ever in New York City history to be sent, along with four other men, to see "Old Sparky," the name given to the electric chair in the notorious Sing-Sing Prison in Ossining, New York.

Becker did not collect the funds himself, but instead used mobsters to collect the money for him. One of those unsavory characters, who later testified against Becker, was Jack Rosenweig, better known by his street name, "Bald Jack Rose." As he became partners with a low-level

"Gyp" Horowitz with captors. The story goes that "Gyp" was caught sitting at the dining room table in his underwear. He asked to be permitted to don a suit before getting arrested. *Courtesy of Library of Congress.*

Gunmen going to Sing-Sing. *Courtesy of Library of Congress.*

Left: Lieutenant "Chas" Becker in uniform. *Courtesy of Library of Congress.*

Below: The Sing-Sing electric chair took nine horrible minutes to execute Becker. *Courtesy of Library of Congress.*

gambler named Harry "Beansy" Rosenthal, things would soon change for Becker.

Rosenthal owned several illicit gambling halls in Times Square. According to an article in *Times News Weekly*, he knew that giving a cut of his earnings to various individuals was the reality of everyday life if one wanted to survive in Times Square. He was fully aware that Becker was someone who accepted bribes in exchange for his protection—he would prohibit police attacks on the shady businesses.

Charles Becker, the only
member of the New York Police
Department to ever be executed.
Some believe he was framed.
Courtesy of Library of Congress.

By handing off payments to Becker, via a collector, and agreeing to take Becker on as a partner, Rosenthal played the game well. However, once Rosenthal caught the attention of Waldo, he forced Becker's hand. The same article reports that Becker searched the home of Rosenthal and claimed that it was an unlawful gambling business. Some members of Rosenthal's family were arrested. The officers did a lot of damage to Rosenthal's home as well as some of their equipment. Rosenthal retaliated by blowing the whistle on Becker and his corrupt ways.

Rosenthal went to the newspapers, and later the district attorney, to describe in detail what life was like with the "men in blue." He claimed that they were supposed to protect their citizens but instead were some of the worst thugs. He also implicated Rose as the collector for Becker.

Becker, sometimes known as Lieutenant Charles or "Chas," became incensed, but probably also worried, when word reached him about the headlines in the papers brought about by Rosenthal's big mouth. He was also concerned that Rosenthal was talking to the district attorney who listened to him intently with political ambition. Becker found out that the gambler was going to testify about the goings-on in Times Square. He had to prevent Rosenthal from doing any more damage.

Warden at Sing-Sing. *Courtesy of Library of Congress.*

"Dago Frank" avoiding cameras. He was quite a bad man and killer. *Courtesy of Library of Congress.*

Gunman on trial. *Courtesy of Library of Congress.*

Later testimony by Rose discussed how a meeting was called in Harlem, which was the headquarters of the Lenox Avenue Gang, the crew for another mobster, Big Jack Zelig. It was here that Becker called for a hit to be made on Rosenthal. He turned to some of the gang members who were well known to him—Rose, along with Harry Vallon, Louis "Bridgey" Webber and Sam Schepps—as well as to various newspapers. They sometimes did horrible acts, such as the one proposed by Becker, for the right price. However, they would botch up this job.

The Lenox Hill Gang consisted mostly of pickpockets, robbers and hoodlums who were hired out for larger crimes such as killing. Its leader was in his mid-twenties, known on the streets as "Gyp the Blood," but his real name was Harry Horowitz. He had a fearsome reputation—he was known to break a randomly picked man's back from on his knee on the first try for a two-dollar bet.

In addition to enlisting Horowitz, Becker had additional associates, who were also members of the gang, to assist with carrying out the hit. These men were "Lefty" Louis Rosenberg, Jacob "Whitey Lewis" Seidenschmer and Francisco "Dago Frank" Cirofici. Rose later testified that he rented a

Body of "Dago Frank" being carried to a hearse after he was electrocuted in Sing-Sing. *Courtesy of Library of Congress.*

gray Packard getaway car, with Willie Shapiro as the driver. It was reported that Becker drew up the plans to be carried out at the Hotel Metropole on West Forty-third Street, near Broadway and Sixth Avenue.

The men arrived at the Hotel Metropole in the early hours of Tuesday morning, July 16, 1912. Rosenthal had been inside eating while another man watched as a lookout from inside the hotel. A messenger was sent inside to tell Rosenthal that he was wanted outside. Once Rosenthal got up to walk out the door, the lookout headed out in front of him. The door swung open, and he gave the sign to the gunmen waiting in the idling gray car with Shapiro behind the wheel. They filed out of the car and fired at Rosenthal as he exited the hotel; the gunmen shot four times until he fell to the ground. One of the assassins finished the job by firing point blank into Rosenthal's head. They all then jumped into the car and raced up Sixth Avenue before vanishing into the darkness.

Unfortunately for Horowitz, many people had seen him during the crime, including witnesses who would later testify that they saw the murder and identified three culprits, including Vallon, Webber and Rose. Shortly after the shooting, in an effort to save himself, Rose spilled his guts—he turned himself in and identified the gunmen as well as the driver. He probably

Above: Waldo, who pushed Becker to rein in Rosenthal. *Courtesy of Library of Congress.*

Right: Harry Vallon. Some believe it was Vallon who pulled the trigger that killed Rosenthal. He probably had a larger role than he let on. *Courtesy of Library of Congress.*

realized that with the involvement of Becker, this case would become much larger than the reputations of the gunmen.

The police began a large-scale manhunt to find the hit men who so brazenly carried out the murder of Rosenthal. Cirofici was arrested within weeks in Harlem with his wife. It was believed, as reported in the *New York Times*, that James Verrella, who owned Dante's Cafe at 163 West Thirty-fourth Street, alerted the police that Cirofici was there. He was killed by associates of Cirofici as revenge.

In August 1912, it was assumed by tips that at least some of the gunmen had bolted north to the Catskills. More specifically, some of the wanted criminals fled to Ulster County as well as to counties surrounding Ulster. Horowitz, Seidenschmer and Vallon were known at some point to have been in/around Ulster. This served to excite the populace of these areas.

In the case of Vallon, he was actually caught in Big Indian, located in Ulster County. He later became an informant, turning in evidence to the state in exchange for immunity from prosecution. Vallon's testimony was instrumental in sending not only the gunmen to the electric chair but also Becker as well. He probably also had a hand in giving up the hiding place of Seidenschmer.

"Whitey Lewis" arriving at Sing-Sing. *Courtesy of Library of Congress.*

"Whitey Lewis," a member of the Lenox Avenue Gang, was part of Zelig's crew. *Courtesy of Library of Congress.*

Seidenschmer, who was one of the gunmen, was caught not too far from where Vallon was apprehended. He was captured in Fleischmanns, just over the border from Ulster, in Greene County. New York City detectives journeyed to Kingston by car and then from Kingston, according to the *New York Times*, took a train to get to Seidenschmer.

Once in custody, Seidenschmer would be taken back to Kingston until the detectives could return to New York City. Ulster County was animated when the manhunt became focused in the Upstate area. It was believed by the New York City Police Department that Horowitz and Rosenberg were probably hiding near Big Indian in Ulster or somewhere just over the border in Green County where Seidenschmer had been discovered working as farmhand.

Taking Officer Becker to jail. *Courtesy of Library of Congress.*

Lieutenant "Chas" Becker and a sheriff taking him to jail. Some historians believe today that Becker should not have gone to the chair; some counter that he was framed by Rose. *Courtesy of Library of Congress.*

Police working the case were alerted to the possibility of Horowitz being in the area because his wife had been seen leaving New York City with another woman, driving toward Upstate New York. At one point, she was even identified by police near Kingston. They were correct; he was not too far away and, in fact, was in Tannersville, a short distance from Ulster County.

The detectives decided to set up watch stations in Shandaken, Big Indian, Pine Hill and over the border in Fleischmanns. Meanwhile, local newspapers picked up on the excitability of the manhunt. Some papers ran stories about citizens in Kingston and Saugerties claiming they had either seen the gunmen or at least spotted their car. One such individual owned the Werner Hotel on the Saugerties-Kingston Road. He called the police when he believed that Horowitz's car passed his business. The police scurried into action and caught up to the reported car; when they pulled it over, its surprised occupants proved that they were not who the police were looking for.

The *Kingston Daily Freeman* ran a story that prominent Kingston residents James Loughran, John Rogers and Philip DeGarmo were camping in Greene

Jail. *Courtesy of Library of Congress.*

County when they claimed that Horowitz, with luggage in tow, asked them for directions to the village of Catskill. Yet another story circulated that Kingston Police Officer Leonard was convinced two men who had a blue car towed to a garage on Clinton Avenue were Horowitz and Rosenberg. He trailed them to the City Hotel on Main Street where they registered.

After continuing to watch them eat at a local establishment, he called for backup to have another officer meet him at the hotel. They spoke with the owner, who tried to convince the police that the people they were asking about were not wanted men but legitimate guests. The officers would hear nothing of it. When they went upstairs to the suspected room, they did not find Horowitz but rather a resident of a local town. After the two officers left the hotel, the owner's son said that they had been knocking on the wrong door. He also claimed, however, that the men in question were not there anyway.

The two men were in the Catskills and, in fact, were in the area where the detectives had focused their attention. However, fearing they would be

Hey! John! Give us a tow? "Lefty Louis" and "Gyp the Blood" are the figures in the rowboat. *Courtesy of Library of Congress.*

Home of "Lefty Louis" and "Gyp the Blood." Both men were not even out of their twenties. *Courtesy of Library of Congress.*

caught, they fled back to New York City, where they were eventually caught in Queens. They were discovered, as detectives had hoped, as a result of trailing the two men's wives. Once seized, the men of the Lenox Avenue Gang were placed on trial, as was Becker.

By the time of the trial, Rose, Vallon, Webber and Shapiro were all being held in the same jail cell with plenty of opportunities to get their stories straight. Their testimony helped send the guys who were the "gun men" to the electric chair. Becker, of the New York City Police Department's Strong Arm Squad, was also indicted in the murder of Rosenthal and was sentenced to die as well, largely as the result of the testimony of his debt collector. He would be remembered as the only New York City police officer ever to be sentenced to be executed. If this was not enough for him to go down in infamy, his electrocution took nine minutes.

CHAPTER 14

The Ulster County Sheriff's Department

Bringing the Wicked to Justice

No book about historic evildoers would be complete without spotlighting those individuals whose job it was to bring the wicked to justice. The Ulster County Sheriff's Department has had a long history of upholding the law, dating back to the 1600s. Criminals were oftentimes as afraid of these officers as they were respectful of them. One such individual was Ulster County Sheriff Zadoc P. Boice.

Boice hailed from the town of Olive in Ulster County—Boiceville, to be exact, where his family had settled. He was born on July 29, 1858. He married Delta Elmendorf, also from Olive, in 1880. They had two daughters, named Lena and Delta.

The future sheriff was the son of Lemuel and Mary Ann Boice. The Boices were originally a farming family who moved into the tanning industry, which was big during the nineteenth century. Their business then morphed into a lumber business, as a direct consequence of tanning, after stripping hemlocks of their barks. Eventually, the Boices moved into mills.

Zadoc Boice did not participate in the family businesses immediately. He did work for his father but then decided he wanted to work for a local hotel. Later, he entered into a partnership with a local grocer. Even at a young age, he was known as honest. After Boice's father passed away, he purchased his dad's real estate interests, which bequeathed him some wealth in 1885.

In 1893, Boice entered political life as a town supervisor; he did so again in 1894. By 1906, this rising young Republican was asked to run for the post of Ulster County sheriff. It is not known if he had any prior law enforcement

Sheriff Boice, one of the more popular Ulster County sheriffs, was greatly respected by both his community and those he tracked down and brought to justice. *Courtesy of Town of Olive clerk's office.*

experience or where he earned his reputation as a sleuth. It might have been because he was an avid hunter and used to track animals.

In an article written in the *New York Tribune*, Boice, called Zack by those who knew him well, was venerated by all of the strata of society. Even though he was a man of some money, he still made sure that he was fair with all, even his workers. When times were not terrific, he made sure to find employment for those who were in need of it.

Boice would be Ulster County sheriff from 1907 to 1909. During that time, he became one of the most feared, yet revered, lawmen. In one of the more sensational criminal cases that seized Ulster County, the culprit, Big Bad Bill Monroe, was almost happy to see Sheriff Boice when he came to take him back to New York from California. Monroe claimed that one of the reasons he did not fight or try to escape was because he respected Boice and felt that he would be fair in his dealings with him. He continued that if anyone else had come to collect him, he would have kept trying to escape until he succeeded or died trying. Even Demetrio Zema seemed to be fond of the sheriff, telling him that he would be back someday—whether this was a threat or a "no hard feelings" type of comment is between Boice and Zema.

Although Boice presided over some of the more memorable criminals in Ulster County, he also had to deal with less-threatening everyday situations like horse theft, which was all too common. One example occurred on Lucas

Kingston Court House. This courthouse functioned for many years as a place to hold both trials and prisoners. *Author's collection.*

Turnpike, involving the milkman E.V. Schoonmaker in the spring of 1909. This turned out to be an active year for the sheriff's department.

On June 3, 1909, Boice was informed by the Horse Protection Association that thieves had struck the barn of Schoonmaker. The thieves had found the barn door unlocked and took a black mare and milk cart with the dealer's name still on the wagon. The thieves made their getaway on the Lucas Turnpike toward Kingston. En route, they forced open another farmer's barn, but for some reason, they were scared away. Once the sheriff was contacted, he notified the various towns, cities and counties on both sides of the Hudson River. This was not always an easy task, as the sheriff's department did not benefit from all of the technology that today's sheriffs and deputies have access to. They did not have computers or cell phones or, in some cases, even patrol cars. Those who drove in patrol cars often encountered roads that were still inaccessible to such vehicles. Thus, the sheriff distributed fliers to get the word out, advertising a $50 reward for the return of the horse and wagon. A larger reward of $100 was offered for the capture of the thieves.

For his efforts, the sheriff earned a salary of about $3,500. He not only pursued thieves and murderers but also even apprehended those who hunted out of season. These individuals were brought to justice—they were fined and their deer, as well as hides, were confiscated.

Things did not always run so smoothly for Boice. He faced at least one embarrassing situation when a convict being held in the Ulster County Jail managed to pick his cell lock with a broom handle. The newspaper reported that Thomas Cosgrove was caught only through the untiring questions of, and leads followed by, Boice. His inquiries began with the guards, who he found fault with, as they did not set the lock properly—a broom handle should not have been able to penetrate it. He also called on all the prisoners in the jail and talked to them privately in his office. What he discovered was that Cosgrove had garnered the cooperation of many of his fellow criminals, that two prisoners even escaped with him and that he had also shared his plans and eventual destination with them all. It had been decided that Cosgrove would cross the river and hide in the woods on the east side of the Hudson River. The other escapees went their own way.

Boice went to his own home on Wall Street in Kingston and used a phone to alert sheriffs in Dutchess County about Cosgrove. Boice sent his right-hand man, Undersheriff George W. Dumond, across the river to help the Dutchess County officers in their pursuit. Cosgrove was caught by Deputy Sheriff Stickles in a local restaurant, quite by accident. He entered the restaurant, and when the man running the counter called out to Stickles, Stickles saw a man shift nervously and refuse to make eye contact with the lawman. Probably having been briefed about what Cosgrove looked like, he became suspicious and asked him if he was the guy who was wanted across the river. Cosgrove stated "No," still not looking the deputy sheriff in the eye. Stickles, believing the similarities were too striking, decided to arrest Cosgrove. He told Boice that he would personally drive over the river to return Cosgrove. Those who were with Boice exclaimed that he smiled for the first time in the days since the escape took place.

A glimpse into the sheriff's demeanor can be gleaned from an exchange caught by a newspaper reporter who was covering the capture of Cosgrove. The first words out of Boice's mouth to Cosgrove were, "Hello Tommy, we're glad you're back." This was followed by: "Lock him up!" Cosgrove winked and replied, "I didn't know you had any locks here." Boice assured Cosgrove that his previous lock-picking stunt was not his fault; he had taught the jailers who were responsible a very valuable lesson that they would not forget. The exchange was concluded with the sheriff asking Cosgrove if he had anything to eat in the days he was gone. The reply was "a few bananas." Boice ordered that the prisoner be given a good meal at once. The year after Cosgrove was caught was also the year that Boice's term came to an end. The next year would be an active one, though, with run-ins with the likes of Monroe and Zema, to name a few.

One of Sheriff Boice's indispensable deputy sheriffs in Ulster County was William Cohen. Many times, it was Cohen who did much patrolling and legwork, especially around areas surrounding the construction of the Ashokan Reservoir, such as Brown's Station. Cohen's life was oftentimes placed in jeopardy; for example, when nothing had turned up during his search of prisoner Samuel Ford's cell, the prompting of a prison stool pigeon led Cohen to find a weapon, but only after it had sliced his hand. There was no doubt that the felon's blade was meant for Cohen.

Not all of the perpetrators that Cohen apprehended were cold-hearted killers or robbers, however. Many of the calls that Cohen had to answer were for drunken disturbances, domestic disputes and, in one instance, from a band of what the local paper described as "gypsies" who were camping nearby. They elicited the help of the deputy sheriff to hunt down a girl and a boy who had eloped. Both families, who were from different camps, wanted them returned. The couple had eloped at least three times in the past.

Cohen was not always a deputy sheriff. He started out life in the clothing business and at one point was a night watchman; he resigned in order to become a law officer. During his tenure as a night watchman, he was noted for helping a police officer save the life of Meyer Friedman and his family. Cohen had seen fire and smoke coming from their home. He rushed into the home of the family, who lived on Fair Street in Kingston, to pull them out of their beds. His reputation for bravery would follow him for the rest of his life.

Cohen was the son of Jewish immigrants. His father, Albert Cohen, was a well-known clothier who had a shop on North Front Street in Kingston. Albert Cohen immigrated to the United States from Germany in 1857, arriving in New York City. Before settling in Kingston, he first went south to Virginia, where he lived for a short period of time. Then Albert Cohen and his wife, Sarah, who also emigrated from Germany, decided to make Kingston their home.

The Cohens resided at number 54 North Front Street. In Kingston, they raised a family of seven children; William was the fourth-oldest child. Before becoming a deputy sheriff, Cohen worked in his father's store. He eventually was married twice: once to a woman named Augusta and at another time, somewhere in between 1900 and 1920, he is listed in a federal census as being married to a woman named Florence. He did not report having any children.

Albert Cohen, and most likely his family, belonged to a synagogue in Kingston named Temple Emanuel. The temple was chartered four years before Albert Cohen migrated to Kingston. In 1905, it would be at this temple where Albert Cohen's funeral would be conducted.

Cohen was not the only member of his family to enter law enforcement. Aaron, his younger brother, became a police commissioner in Kingston. Aaron Cohen, however, did not achieve the accolades that his brother did for bringing the wicked to justice.

One of the more infamous criminals that Cohen brought to justice was Roscoe W. Ney. Ney caught the attention of Kingston when he tried several times to kill his wife, Freida. He claimed he was going to shoot her and went as far as pulling out a pistol. After one instance when he actually physically attacked his wife, Ney's neighbors finally intervened and had him arrested. After he went to trial, Ney was judged to be insane and was committed to the Middletown Asylum.

Ney was only at the asylum for a short time before he was able to escape and went on the run in September 1907. On a few occasions, he called the home of his wife to harass her and continue to threaten her life. Cohen was sent to the Ney residence on Pearl Street in Kingston to protect Mrs. Ney. Eventually, Ney was caught when he turned himself in to police in Norwalk, Connecticut. He was heading back to Middletown by the end of September 1907.

During his time as an Ulster County deputy sheriff, Cohen was described in various newspapers as a respected sleuth and a modern-day Sherlock Holmes. He had an innate ability not only to anticipate the moves of criminals but also to track them down. Later in his life, newspapers wished him well when he was hit by a motorcycle while crossing the street. It was feared that he was dead, but he fortunately emerged with only some minor scratches.

If it was law enforcement's job to bring the wicked to justice, it was the jailer's job to guard the wicked. When Boice became Ulster County sheriff, he asked the then commissioner of highways, Seth Jocelyn, to become the county jailer at the Ulster County Jail. He was to take that position on January 1, 1906. Jocelyn's job was to keep order in the jail and also to make sure that contraband did not enter its walls. In one newspaper account, it became a problem for prisoners' friends and families to sneak liquor into the jail.

Things did go wrong at the jails, however, such as Cosgrove's lock-picking escape, which was an embarrassment to the jailer. Still another spectacle was when an Ellenville police officer journeyed through Kingston with a prisoner who had been charged with drunken disorderly conduct. The officer was on his way to Albany to drop off the prisoner when he stopped by the Ulster County Jail. As he was met by Jocelyn, it was discovered that the officer had lost the key to his handcuffs. After looking for the key and even trying to snake the prisoner out of the handcuffs, Jocelyn was forced to fetch a hammer and spent a considerable amount of time breaking the cuffs off of the man's wrists.

If that was not amusing enough, Jocelyn once had to deal with an individual who seemed to be trying to break in to the jail. The individual was finally shown the way out of the jail, for it was discovered that he was not trying to get inside, but in fact had become lost and disoriented in the adjacent courthouse. He believed that somehow he had ended up in jail and was calling to be let out.

References

BOOKS

Beers, J.H. *Commemorative Biographical Record of Ulster County, N.Y.: Containing Biographical Sketches of Prominent and Representative Citizens, and of Many of the Early Settled Families*. Chicago: J.H. Beers & Co, 1896.

Burgess, Larry E. *Mohonk, Its People and Spirit: A History of One Hundred and Forty Years of Growth and Service*. Fleischmanns, NY: Purple Mountain Press, 2009.

Clinton, George. *Public Papers of George Clinton, First Governor of New York 1777–1795, 1801–1804*. Hugh Hastings, editor. Albany: State of New York, 1899.

Conley, Sheldon. *The Battle of Fort Montgomery: A Short History*. Fleischmanns, NY: Purple Martin Press, 2002.

Hasbrouck, Abraham. "Diary and Scrapbook (1734–1846)." In *Earliest Records of the Hasbrouck Family in America with European Background*, compiled by Kenneth E. Hasbrouck. New Paltz, NY: Hasbrouck Family Association and Huguenot Historical Society, 1992.

Hasbrouck, Kenneth E., comp. *The Hasbrouck Family in America with European Background*. Vols. 1 and 2, 3rd edition. New Paltz, NY: Huguenots Historical Society, 1986.

Lefevre, Ralph. *History of New Paltz and its Old Families from 1678 to 1820*. Albany, NY: Fort Orange Press, 1903.

Pratt, George W. *An Account of the British Expedition above the Highlands and the Events Connected with the Burning of Kingston in 1777.* Marbletown, NY: Ulster County Historical Society, 1977.

Ruttenber, E.M. *History of the Town of Newburgh.* Newburgh, NY: E.M. Ruttenber & Sons, Printer, 1859.

Schenkman, A.J. *Washington's Headquarters in Newburgh: Home to a Revolution.* Charleston, SC: The History Press, 2008.

Schoonmaker, Marius. *The History of Kingston, New York from its Early Settlements to the Year 1820.* New York: Burr Printing House, 1888.

Steuding, Bob. *The Last of the Handmade Dams: The Story of the Ashokan Reservoir.* Fleischmanns, NY: Purple Mountain Press, 1985.

CENSUS

U.S. Bureau of the Census. *U.S. Census of Population.* Washington, DC: Government Printing Office, 1880, 1900, 1910, 1920.

NEWSPAPERS AND PERIODICALS

Amsterdam Evening Recorder and Daily Democrat. "Craft Found Guilty of Murder in Second Degree." May 18, 1910.

———. "Jumped Through Window and Landed on His Head." May 11, 1910.

Auburn Citizen. "Tried Twice to Escape." May 11, 1910.

Brooklyn NY Daily Star. "Bury Two in Mt. Zion." April 14, 1914.

Clinton New York Advertiser. "Razor Convicts a Slayer." October 9, 1909.

Evening Post. "Chauffeur Sentenced for Murder." May 13, 1910.

Kingston Daily Freeman. "Accused of Firing Woods." October 24, 1911.

———. "Aged Undertaker Under Arrest." January 31, 1912.

———. "A.K. Smiley Ill." August 23, 1907.

———. "Appeal Taken in Craft Case." July 27, 1911.

———. "Argument Not Completed." October 17, 1910.

———. "Ashokan Saloon Men Indicted." October 25, 1909.

———. "Awaiting A Verdict in the Zema Case." October 21, 1909.

———. "Bad Bill Monroe." December 7, 1908.

———. "Bad Bill Monroe Back to Dannemora." July 24, 1912.

———. "Bad Bill Monroe Gets an Airing." March 23, 1909.

————. "Bad Bill Monroe Seeks Liberty." May 29, 1912.

————. "Bad Bill Monroe Starts Prison Row." June 24, 1912.

————. "Bad Bill Monroe's California Escape." July 23, 1909.

————. "Becker Trial Begins Today." October 7, 1912.

————. "Becker Trial Still in Progress." October 17, 1912.

————. "Bill Made Threats Week Before the Crime." January 19, 1910.

————. "Bill Monroe a Letter Writer." August 31, 1908.

————. "Bill Monroe Glad to be at Home." December 26, 1909.

————. "Bill Monroe Goes West." June 9, 1909.

————. "Bill Monroe in Orange County." September 3, 1908.

————. "Bill Monroe is on Trial." January 18, 1910.

————. "Bill Monroe May Be Caught." September 26, 1908.

————. "Bill Monroe's Brother." October 24, 1908.

————. "Black Hand Case Against Zema." October 21, 1909.

————. "Bringing Bill Back." November 27, 1909.

————. "The Burglars." October 12, 1881.

————. "Carman Realizes His Position." February 5, 1912.

————. "Carman Said to Be Worth 100,000 Dollars." February 1, 1912.

————. "Carman Sent to Middletown." February 1, 1912.

————. "Carman's Prosperous Year." December 23, 1912.

————. "Chauffeur of Murder Car Offered Bribe." November 4, 1912.

————. "Confesses to Firing the Forest." November 20, 1911.

————. "A Courageous Sheriff." *Volume 02*, October 30 1903.

————. "Craft Indicted First Degree." June 14, 1909.

————. "Craft Murder Trial Tangle." December 18, 1909.

————. "Craft Sentenced to Dannemora." May 13, 1910.

————. "Delford Van Leuven Guilty." November 22, 1911.

————. "Detective Work in Plumland." July 10, 1909.

————. "Eight Jurors for Craft Trial." May 10, 1909.

————. "Eloquent Plea for Mercy to Zema." October 22, 1909.

————. "Evidence Points to Lt. Becker." July 30, 1912.

————. "The Fallon Inquest." June 11, 1909.

————. "Fallon Inquest Held Saturday." June 7, 1909.

————. "Fannie Toth was Surprised." October 1, 1908.

————. "Fatal Shooting at Lattingtown." May 28, 1909.

————. "Five Arraigned on Murder Charges." August 22, 1912.

————. "Ford Appeal Taken." October 23, 1909.

————. "Ford Finds Fault." October 4, 1909.

————. "Ford Murder Trial." September 21, 1909.

————. "Ford Murder Trial." September 27, 1909.

————. "Ford Murder Trial Appeal Argued." October 14, 1910.

————. "Ford Murder Trial: Six Jurors Selected up to this Afternoon." September 23, 1909.

————. "Ford's Murder Trial." September 20, 1909.

————. "Ford's Story Cross Examined." September 30, 1909.

————. "Friendly Old Gentleman Tried Hard to Break Into the Ulster County Jail." June 11, 1909.

————. "Game of Catching Gyp the Blood." August 8, 1912.

————. "Gardiner Bad Man Still at Large." August 24, 1908.

————. "Grand Jury to Work." November 2, 1910.

————. "Gunman Found Guilty of Murder in the First Degree." November 19, 1912.

————. "Gunman's Sentence Next Tuesday." November 20, 1912.

————. "Gunmen Arrive at Sing-Sing." November 26, 1912.

————. "Gunmen Convicted of Rosenthal Murder." November 21, 1912.

————. "Gunmen Did Not Try to Hide." September 12, 1912.

————. "Gunmen Plead Not Guilty." September 18, 1912.

————. "Gyp the Blood in Various Places." August 24, 1912.

————. "Gyp the Blood Tells His Story." November 14, 1912.

————. "High Falls Cops are Not Tanks." October 3, 1908.

————. "Horse Thieves on Lucas Turnpike." June 3, 1909.

————. "I Congratulate You Said Becker." October 14, 1912.

————. "I'll Come Back Says Demetrio." October 23, 1909.

————. "Incendiary Fire at Kerhonkson." June 3, 1909.

————. "Indictments in Rosenthal Case." August 21, 1912.

————. "Informer Rose Enjoys his First Day of Freedom." November 23, 1912.

————. "Insurance Company to Sue Carman." July 10, 1912.

————. "Jail Lock Picked with Broken Broom Handle." July 23, 1908.

————. "Jocelyn to become Jailer." December 15, 1906.

————. "Judge Fitts Dead in Bed." December 17, 1909.

————. "Lake Mohonk Robbers." September 17, 1895.

————. "Let's Go Set the Woods on Fire." November 21, 1911.

————. "Local Death Record." December 17, 1912.

————. "Locked to Prisoner." February 26, 1909.

————. "Mayor M'Clellan Will Testify." September 21, 1912.

————. "May Return to Italy." October 22, 1909.

————. "Monroe Gets Twenty Years." November 21, 1923.

————. "More Badness by Bill Monroe." May 11, 1910.

————. "Mountain Bandits of Long Ago." June 3, 1916.

————. "Murder Car Driver Will be Set Free." November 20, 1912.

————. "Murder Case Goes to Jury." May 12, 1910.

————. "Murder Paymaster Gives Testimony." October 15, 1912.

————. "Mr. Hepworth not Gyp the Blood." August 23, 1912.

————. "Mrs. Bill Monroe is Back Home." August 27, 1908.

————. "Ney Heard from by Telephone." September 19, 1907.

————. "Ney in Custody." September 24, 1907.

————. "Ney Saw a Lawyer." August 12, 1907.

————. "Not Bill Monroe." November 7, 1908.

————. "Off to Dannemora." March 29, 1910.

————. "Police Find Lefty's Pistol." August 3, 1912.

————. "Police May Have Gunman's Letters." September 16, 1912.

————. "Prisoners Plead in County Court." November 14, 1911.

————. "Roscoe Ney Insane." August 12, 1907.

————. "Rose Tells How Becker Ordered Rosenthal Slain." October 12, 1912.

————. "Selecting Craft Jury." December 16, 1909.

————. "Shapiro Offers Full Confession." October 28, 1912.

————. "Sheriffs After Bad Bill Monroe." December 4, 1909.

————. "Suicide of Roscoe W. Ney." October 28, 1908.

————. "Taken to Asylum." September 25, 1907.

————. "300 Dollar Reward for Monroe is Up." September 4, 1908.

————. "Toth Case Adjourned." October 2, 1908.

————. "Van Leuven Pleaded Guilty." December 5, 1911.

————. "Walter Kruse Sees Gunmen." September 16, 1912.

————. "Where did Rich Policeman Get It?" August 10, 1912.

————. "Whitman Offers 5,000 Dollar Reward." August 16, 1912.

————. "Who Pay for the Ford Murder Trial?" February 12, 1912.

————. "Zema Case Affirmed." December 6, 1911.

————. "Zema Dynamite Case on Trial." October 26, 1909.

————. "Zema Sentenced for 12 to 15 Years." October 23, 1909.

————. "Zema's Letter from Black Hand Leader." October 23, 1909.

Levine, David. "Sing Sing Prison, Ossining, NY: A History of Hudson Valley's Jail Up the River." *Hudson Valley Magazine*, September 12, 2011.

Newburgh Daily Journal. "The Craft Murder Case Will Be Tried Again in Ulster County." February 17, 1910.

————. "A Curious Complication over a Judge's Death." December 18, 1909.

————. "Henry Craft Found Guilty." May 13, 1910.

Newburgh Telegram. "Republicans Nominated Zadoc Boice." July 7, 1906.

————. "Young Craft Well Known in Newburgh." May 14, 1910.

New Haven Register. "Thefts by Wholesale: Lyman Freer as He Called Himself Had a Long Reach." October 31, 1896.

New York Herald. "Condemned Man was Armed." October 2, 1909.

————. "Situations Wanted." April 4, 1903.

New York Times. "Aboriginal Ulster." September 16, 1906.

————. "Along the Line with the Aqueduct Police." April 4, 1909.

————. "Aqueduct Police." April 4, 1909.

————. "Bad Man Gets Away." August 25, 1908.

————. "Bad Man of Orange Beats 6, and Burns Barn." August 23, 1908.

————. "Bill Monroe Dons Skirts." September 5, 1908.

————. "Bill Monroe is Elusive." August 31, 1908.

————. "Burglars Pleading Guilty." April 16, 1880.

————. "City to be Built at Ashokan Dam." September 7, 1908.

————. "Clue to Gyp the Blood." August 13, 1912.

————. "Confessed Slayer May Be Innocent." November 1, 1925.

————. "Convict Stabs Guard." June 24, 1912.

————. "Crime and its Penalty." June 21, 1879.

————. "Dougherty Gets Murder Witness." July 28, 1912.

————. "Find Gyp the Blood's Wife." August 7, 1912.

————. "Find Lefty Louie in the Catskills." August 4, 1912.

————. "Frontier Camp Close to the City's Border." January 1, 1910.

————. "Gambler Who Defied Police is Shot Dead." July 16, 1912.

————. "Gyp and Lefty Caught Right Here in Town." September 15, 1912.

————. "Jack Rose Held: Auto Owners Seek for Terms." July 19, 1912.

————. "Kill Betrayer of Dago Frank." July 31, 1912.

————. "Lawless Camps." January 9, 1910.

————. "Model Camp Built at Ashokan Dam." May 2, 1909.

————. "Mountain Hunt Goes On." August 8, 1912.

————. "New Clue in the Catskills." August 14, 1912.

————. "Posse Gets Fugitives Accused of Murder." August 2, 1923.

————. "A Republican Slate Broken." October 10, 1894.

————. "Searching for Monroe." August 24, 1908.

————. "Shawangunk Burglars." December 11, 1881.

————. "Sullivan There When Rosenthal was Shot Down." July 27, 1912.

————. "Surprised at Card Game." August 25, 1912.

————. "Think Prisoner is Monroe." September 10, 1908.

————. "300 Dead in Aqueduct's Way." June 2, 1909.

————. "Van Winkle in Real Life." April 16, 1897.

————. "Whitey Lewis Caught Upstate on Tip of Vallon." August 2, 1912.

NY Union News. "Four Gunmen Electrocuted." April 1914.

Ostego Farmer. "In Central New York." August 20, 1915.

Pine Plains Register. The Register. July 28, 1905.

————. The Register. November 1, 1907.

Poughkeepsie Daily Eagle. "Ashokan Dam Murder Case Argued." December 1, 1910.

————. "Blame Police for Murderous Escape." August 22, 1912.

Times News Weekly. "Old-Fashioned Police Work Ended Manhunt For Movie-Fan Murderers." November 5, 2009.

Watertown Daily Times. "Pocket Piece Led to Man's Conviction." September 30, 1909.

About the Author

A.J. Schenkman is an educator of history in the Hudson Valley and a volunteer firefighter. He has written extensively on the histories of Ulster and Orange Counties and is the author of two books and numerous articles on Washington's Headquarters in Newburgh. Currently, he is featured each month in two columns on Ulster and Orange County histories.

Also by A.J. Schenkman:
Washington's Headquarters in Newburgh: Home to a Revolution

Visit us at
www.historypress.net